PRAISE FOR *EVERY LITTLE WIN*

"What if the very things we thought would sink us are the things meant to build us into who we were made to be? In their very candid and vulnerable book, Todd and Brooke lay it all bare, sharing the real and raw ups and downs of their lives. This is to point readers not to what they have overcome but to the One who can make all things new. *Every Little Win* is a beautiful, heartfelt invitation for all of us to embrace our story and to find real lasting hope no matter what we've faced."

—PATRICK AND RUTH SCHWENK, AUTHORS OF *IN A BOAT IN THE MIDDLE OF A LAKE: TRUSTING THE GOD WHO MEETS US IN OUR STORM* AND HOSTS OF *ROOTLIKE FAITH* PODCAST

"If you've ever had a dream yet to be realized or struggled to see a clear path to victory in your life, get ready to be encouraged. Todd and Brooke Tilghman know exactly how you feel. Their story will inspire you to keep trying, and in trying, discover that God has a plan and a purpose for every part of your story."

—HEIDI ST. JOHN, BESTSELLING AUTHOR OF *BECOMING MOMSTRONG: HOW TO FIGHT WITH ALL THAT'S IN YOU FOR YOUR FAMILY AND YOUR FAITH* AND HOST OF *OFF THE BENCH WITH HEIDI ST. JOHN* PODCAST

EVERY
LITTLE WIN

EVERY
LITTLE WIN

How Celebrating Small Victories

Can Lead to Big Joy

TODD & BROOKE TILGHMAN
WITH TRICIA GOYER

NELSON
BOOKS

An Imprint of Thomas Nelson

To Eagan, Asher, Shepard, Judah, Olive,
Hosea, Louie, and Wilhelmina.
You all have given us such indescribable joy.
Being your mama and daddy is the big win.

Contents

Prelude

I couldn't hear my own footsteps as I walked onto the Hollywood stage, maybe due to the loud thumping of my heart. Auditorium lights were dim, and the faces in the crowd indistinguishable. Yet I could feel their eyes on me. And even though I sang for that audience, the opinions of four coaches sitting in red chairs would determine if I would be part of this internationally viewed singing competition.

Megastars Nick Jonas, John Legend, Blake Shelton, and Kelly Clarkson sat with their backs to me. The turn of one chair would impact the course of the coming weeks—and maybe even years. Everyone knew that. Yet, as I paused in the middle of the stage, noting the pinpricks of spotlights that broke through the darkness, I knew I had already changed. When it comes to a competition like this, everyone is focused on who's the favorite and which singer they think is going to win the show. Deep down, just by being on this stage, my soul had already claimed a win. Even without one chair turn, a transformation had already happened in my heart.

If you're reading this book, you no doubt know the end of the story. Maybe you journeyed with me through season 18 of *The Voice*. Or perhaps you first heard my singing in a video clip shared on YouTube or Facebook. Some may believe that when I sang "We've Got Tonight" and four chairs turned, things changed. But I'm here to tell you that *The Voice* stage isn't where the biggest change happened. The fact that I was a pastor from deep in the Bible Belt, standing on a Hollywood stage, and singing a secular song proved that I was a different man than when I first started seeking God as a teen. For years I'd been so focused on doing everything right that I didn't give much thought to what God wanted to do with my life. Turns out, he had a few things in mind for me, things I've been happy to discover.

You might have picked up this book thinking it's a story about a pastor's sudden rise to fame. Instead, it's a book about a journey from fear to freedom. Brooke and I didn't set out to make a major discovery, but as we've faced the ups and downs in life, we've observed that the way to move from fear to freedom—and from freedom to joy—is to celebrate all the little wins in life, especially the wins we often forget to notice.

A "win" can be choosing to stand in line to audition for a television show, or it can be sitting down to talk things out with your spouse instead of turning and stomping away. Wins happen every day, but we often forget to notice them. It turns out the simple saying "count your blessings" is really where everything changes. At the end of the day, when we look for our wins and celebrate them, things start to change. *We* start to change. And each of us can take this journey.

My wife, Brooke, and I have been married twenty-two years, and we've overcome more fears than we can count. We've been at the brink of divorce, have had a critically ill child, and have struggled to make ends meet (always). Brooke was bound by anxiety and depression for years, and it's a battle she still fights. She'll tell her story about that within these pages.

Brooke and I also pastored a small Mississippi church for over a decade, and no matter what anyone says, pastoring isn't easy. There were always good times in pastoring, but there was also so much that was a struggle. Some people believed we didn't do things right, while others extended kindness.

We adopted two beautiful girls internationally when doing so was impossible on a pastor's salary. We're raising eight kids, each with unique personalities and struggles, which is a full-time job all in itself. On paper, our lives look very full but hardly remarkable—unless you look for the small wins.

Huge achievements get noticed. But if Brooke and I had waited around to find joy until we got a big win, we would have missed out on the amazing life we've lived. Instead, we've found triumph in the mundane. Even in the middle of our hardships, we've sought—and clung to—God's goodness. This has brought happiness in our everyday lives and also allowed us to dare to try for bigger wins. Each step of fighting the fear, and looking for the win, brought us to where we are today. Not only did seeking small joys pave the way to every bigger step, these joys also built up hope within us until it was hard to contain.

As I sang on *The Voice* stage, the joy came bubbling out. Blake Shelton called my bounce "a holy hop." I call it joy in God's goodness. As I sang, thankfulness welled up within me until I couldn't hold it in. That moment was a bright light after a dark road of suffering, and I think it'll help you better understand the joy of this journey if we talk a bit about the suffering first.

I wrote the words below in my journal in 2017 during a particularly difficult season in our lives—before *The Voice*, before I had a number-one song on iTunes. This gives you a glimpse of what God was doing in my heart:

Suffering is kind of an odd thing. It's something we can all relate to, but each person's suffering is uniquely theirs. I have been in full-time ministry since I was eighteen years old, which has given me some perspective on suffering. And this I know most of all: when someone is breaking, no matter why, it hurts.

Too often we fall prey to the puffed-up pride that says, "You think that's bad? Wait until you hear what I went through!" Don't do that. Don't minimize someone else's pain, and don't allow their circumstances to minimize yours.

I don't pastor a megachurch, and (so far) no tracks on iTunes. I don't have a whole bunch of degrees. Here's what I do have. The same thing as you, maybe: a bunch of years of experience dealing with my own pain and the pain of others.

The truth is that even though Brooke and I have ministered in a little Mississippi church for many years, and we have a bunch of kids, we're probably not a whole lot different than you. We know what it is to suffer. We know what it is to break. We can tell you stories of bending every which way to show someone the love of Jesus only to have them step right on your face.

I ended the journal entry noting "two important things to grasp":

Your suffering isn't forever. Your suffering isn't for nothing.

When I came across that entry not long after I won *The Voice*, I chuckled, especially at the line "(So far) no tracks on iTunes." Even back then, I was considering I might do a little something with music. I was dabbling with writing a few songs and trying to record them myself. Never could I have imagined that just a few years later I'd have two songs on iTunes: one sung with Blake Shelton and also an original, "Long Way Home," that made it to number one on the iTunes chart. And since you're reading these words a bit beyond 2017, I'm going to add a couple more important things to my list:

1. Suffering can cause us to face our greatest fears and discover God there, even during painful moments.
2. Freedom and joy come when we look for the little wins in everyday life. Things might not change, but our perspectives can. Even though we may not see how anything good can come out of our circumstances, looking for the little wins leads us to trust God with the bigger story of our lives.

Right now, your heart may be breaking. You might have just buried a spouse, a parent, or a child. You could be in the hellacious firestorm of divorce, or maybe you've filed for bankruptcy, or perhaps you feel like you're walking through wet cement every day just to make it to bedtime. Brooke and I want to share our personal stories in hope that you'll gain a better perspective of *your story*. We don't share these things to draw attention to ourselves. Instead, we want to draw attention to God and all he's done in times we've suffered and in times we've celebrated. We feel this is especially important these days when suffering has been highlighted in nearly every news story from New York City to Meridian, Mississippi, and far beyond.

No one expected 2020 to turn out like it did. We didn't have "global pandemic" penciled in on our calendars. And as the calendar has flipped over to a new year, deep holes of isolation are only being matched by stockpiles of fear. Like no other time in history, we're all going through a different type of suffering.

Suffering normally doesn't send a "save the date." But if you're in the middle of it, that doesn't mean you did anything wrong. Things happen in the world, and to us personally, that don't make sense. But even in the middle of it all, good things can happen. I'm living proof of that. So many have told me that my singing—during *The Voice* and after—has brought them joy during a very hard time. I'm thankful.

I'm thankful that I was given this amazing platform from which to sing, and that I have a dedicated wife and eight kids cheering me on. It all seems like a miracle to me—especially since my marriage to Brooke nearly failed before it hardly got started. Without us together we would have missed out on the family we have, both kids born and those adopted.

Looking at the odds, and our past, Brooke and I shouldn't be together. We've been at the breaking point, but instead of giving up, we pushed through to discover it's so much better on the other side. I've said from the pulpit a hundred times: I would never want to go through all the pain of facing divorce again, but I also wouldn't take a million dollars to have never lived it. It was worth more than I can say. The pain and the suffering taught us about each other, about God, about restoration, and about how good marriage really can be. And that's just one of the biggies. There have been many potholes on our journey.

I held tight to the goodness of God in 2017—after many hard years of suffering—even when I wasn't in the spotlight. Then, God gave me a chance to share his goodness to over seven million people, through music and song and even without words. Freedom and joy have a way of exploding out of us, making others take notice. And that's what happened onstage at *The Voice*.

My songs and my joy have gained many people's attention. My smile and holy hop have caused people to lean in. Many people said they were drawn to the genuineness of this ordinary pastor from Mississippi, which stirred up interest in what Brooke and I have to say. And we don't take this lightly. We've prayed about what to share and how to share it.

Some parts of our story are plainer to see. I lost 110 pounds a few years back, finding a sense of freedom from food addiction, but my eating and health is still something of which I have to be aware. We have two Korean daughters, and like many people who want to adopt, we had to depend on the financial giving of family, friends, and strangers to bring our girls home. This came after Brooke's many years of praying for a daughter once we'd had our three wonderful boys.

Other parts of our story aren't highlighted on social media. We've struggled with family relationships, and our kids have been hurt by people we've trusted. We've been wounded and blessed by the church, and we've no doubt wounded and blessed others too. God has done a lot of work there. He's been faithful.

Yet perhaps the biggest changes have happened within our hearts. For most of my life, one of my biggest motivators was making church people happy. Looking back, I see my insecurities and how a lack of understanding of God's desires for my life caused me to be a people pleaser. I served in ways I thought a godly man should serve, deep down hoping I was doing *good enough*.

I've been a worship leader, youth pastor, and pastor, yet even in my efforts to serve God, there were some seasons when I was just going through the motions. There were other seasons when my pride pushed me to strive for perfection, and then I fell flat on my face when I couldn't achieve it. And even as I tried to give my all, I usually believed it was never enough.

In recent years, my biggest struggle was with the discontent in my heart that dreamed of "something else" besides pastoring. It's not that my life was horrible. Not even close. Yet there was a stirring inside that told me I wanted more. It's a stirring I fought against. After all, the Bible says that "godliness with contentment is great gain" (1 Tim. 6:6).

If my wife heard me talk about "doing something different" once, she heard it a thousand times. Yet even though the inner pull for something more was there, the sensible part of me usually took over. I was a preacher's kid who became a worship leader at sixteen, a youth pastor at eighteen, an associate pastor at thirty, and then—when my father left the pulpit—the head pastor of our church. As a father of eight children, on the salary of a small church, daily life was meager, and I didn't think I should or could do anything else to put food on the table. Still, there was something inside me that said things could be different. I just had no idea how.

Even when I filled out the paperwork and was given a slot for the Atlanta auditions for *The Voice*, I didn't think going was worth the drive. *How could anything come of it?* As I stood in line for hours with thousands of other hopefuls, I was frustrated—with the line, with the waste of time, but mostly with myself. *Why couldn't I just be satisfied?*

Looking back, this was all part of my journey from fear to faith. And then from faith to joy. Fear says: "If we aren't satisfied with where God has us, we have a problem within us." But faith says something different: "Maybe those inner nudges of dissatisfaction are actually from God. Maybe he's wanting us to look to him for something more." And that something more has brought more joy than I can describe.

From the time I was a child, I've had a song on my lips. And during this dark, difficult time in our country's history—a pandemic, natural disasters, and heartbreaking racial injustices—maybe God had a plan. A plan to use me and the songs that I sang to give people hope. A plan to remind me that faith sometimes is just stepping onto the stage that God has prepared.

And maybe now, it's time for me to encourage *you* in that too.

———•———

Often a day—or a season—passes, and we easily paste labels on it like *good* or *bad, easy* or *difficult*. It's not until a big life change happens, and we take time to reflect, that we begin to understand that some good was happening in the middle of the bad or some growing was going on even when things were difficult.

Brooke and I have done a lot of contemplating lately. The win on *The Voice* made us take more notice of all the little wins that have happened along the way—things that didn't seem too important at the time prepared us for the life changes to come.

Since most of life isn't marked by scoreboards or report cards, sometimes we forget to look for the wins. Many times it seems our lives are lacking. When we scan social media, we find that everyone appears to have their acts together except us. We compare our old cars to someone's new one and feel insufficient. Another person's job promotion can cause dissatisfaction in our hearts. Yet we all know the truth: money doesn't equal happiness, and those who seem to have it all are often hurting the most and hiding it. But things change when we take note of the wins in life.

Some wins, like coming in first in a national singing competition, are obvious. But there are tons more that we often don't notice. Brooke and I will point out these wins that we can see clearly now, even when they were hardly noticeable at the time. We encourage you to do the same. But how?

1. Gratitude helps you take note of wins. Focus on what is good. Focus on what God is doing, even in the midst of hard stuff. Stop comparing and appreciate that you are a work in progress. Be thankful for the little things and big things alike.

2. The wins in our lives are often tied to the growing relationships in our lives. When we take time to listen and care for others, we often find ourselves listened to and cared for.

3. We win when we understand that our stories matter. We can look for purpose in the pain. We can find meaning even in heartache. A shift in perspective changes everything, and small celebrations along the way can lead to big wins in our minds, hearts, and lives.

WINS FOR TODAY

✓ We win when we focus on God. When fear says there is something wrong with us, faith reminds us that God loves us so much he wants to give us the desires of our hearts—and he wants *all* of us.

✓ We win when we believe that God has good plans for us.

✓ We win when we understand God's love isn't dependent on us doing everything right.

✓ We win when we face our greatest suffering, or greatest fear, and can still see glimpses of God's goodness there.

✓ We win when we look for one blessing, *even one*, to count today.

CHAPTER I

The Start of a Story and a Song

TODD

I was born into a soulfulness that comes from community, church, and common adversity. I don't remember this, but I'm told that when I was just a toddler, I'd play Matchbox cars on the wrinkled blankets of my granddaddy's bed in the weeks before his death. And it was during that time, at my granddaddy's side, when a country preacher spoke a seed of a promise that has grown into full bloom forty years later. What most of my family saw as a toddler's humming, God stirred within that preacher's heart as something more at work. I like knowing that my granddaddy got to be a part of that.

My granddaddy, Horace James Tilghman—whom everyone called Big Daddy—was born in 1891. He was a farmer on the Mississippi Delta his whole life. My Granny Louise was his second wife, after his first wife's passing. Big Daddy had grown kids when they married, and they had two more together: my dad, Clarence, and my aunt, Brenda. Dad was born when Big Daddy was sixty-five years old. I wasn't yet three when Big Daddy passed, but I have vague memories of him sitting in this high-back black chair that looked like leather. But that was before his stroke. After that, he was in a hospital bed at his house—the one I would climb up on to play. Sometimes I'd stand next to his bed and "sing."

I'm told that even in diapers, I'd rock side to side and hum.

As I moved from one side to the next, I'd hit a note and then sway back and hit it again. As I got a bit older, I'd do the same as I ate. I'd lean forward, hum, take a bite. Lean back and hum as I chewed. I'm sure my mama loved that.

I was at the foot of Big Daddy's bed, swaying and humming, when the preacher, Hulon Evans, came by for a visit. Before he left, he looked down at me and said, "That boy has a special anointing to sing."

Big Daddy only lived a few more weeks after that, and my dad tells me that during his last days on earth, Big Daddy got glimpses of heaven. As he stared up at the ceiling, his eyes saw something more.

"Oh, look at those fields," he'd tell my dad. "Look at those crops. I've never seen crops like that." Seems fitting for a farmer. And it seems fitting that seed of promise for my singing future was planted at Big Daddy's bedside.

I don't remember Pastor Evans's words about my special anointing, but I do remember standing near the altar of Granny Louise's church singing a "special," a solo in front of the whole congregation, at age eight. Pastor Evans must've been proud to see his prophecy taking root, because when I was done with my song, he picked me up and gave me a kiss, and I knew I'd done well. The church folks had a tender way of encouraging kids like me to be involved. Church wasn't just some place I attended; it shaped who I was, especially with regard to music.

Many things come to mind when people think of Mississippi. Cotton fields, muddy waters, and the rhythm of trains on firefly nights. Old men sitting on benches in front of the courthouse, shooting the breeze. Old women in floral dresses, clutching Bibles to their chests as they sit in pews, amen-ing the visiting evangelist. People who are familiar with the South understand that the rise and fall of sharp-note hymns and the high and low cadence of a preacher's sermon are as much a part of life as the orchestra of crickets and katydids when the moon rises.

Now, unless you grew up in a southern church environment, there are a few more terms you may not be familiar with. In the Church of God, the denomination in which I grew up and served—and in many other evangelical and pentecostal denominations—to have a special *anointing* means that God has enabled you for a unique purpose in your life. And if you are part of the congregation, you're called *Brother* or *Sister* out of respect for older adults in the church. As I was growing up, these folks were like family. We had a feeling of kinship with one another. It's like having a whole lotta aunts and uncles who keep tabs on you in the best way possible.

The language of the church was as foundational to my childhood (and my life) as hot summer days, pecan pies, and singing hymns like "Blessed Assurance" and "What a Friend We Have in Jesus." I grew up knowing what things were acceptable and what things could get me into trouble. Rock music, television shows that depicted kids being disrespectful to parents, and going to the movies without my folks were off-limits.

Brooke says, for her, *He-Man and the Masters of the Universe* wasn't allowed, probably because the true master of the universe is Jesus, and no one wanted their kids to get confused. Smurfs were bad too. Some preachers said the *Smurfs* cartoon had satanic themes, and we knew better than to question this logic.

Maybe it's just my personality, but growing up, I felt like a lot of people were trying to scare me to Jesus. Even though church leaders taught me that Jesus loved me, at times there was a "turn or burn" mentality in the things I heard. That's what makes my story—this story—one about transformation. I've overcome the burden of trying to do everything right, and instead I simply follow where God leads me and share the love of Jesus the best I can. And, as you'll read in this book, it's been a process.

My stepping onto the stage at *The Voice* and singing a song that isn't played on Christian radio is a clear example of the freedom I've found from the legalism I felt, though it was largely self-imposed. I've found the freedom to know that God's love isn't contingent on whether or not I do things right—or if I do them good enough. I can fall and fail, and God won't love me less. I've learned that over the years.

Jesus himself was born into obscurity. He slept in a manger, and those who came to see him first—the shepherds—were some of the dirtiest, stinkiest, and poorest people of all. I don't think God sent his only Son to be born in a stable, perform all those miracles, and then die on the cross just to keep us out of hell. I think God did all that so we could know him and because he loves us. His sacrifice was about *here*, not just the *hereafter*.

Learning this has given me great joy that I long to share with those inside and outside the walls of a church. After winning *The Voice*, I'm now able to connect with all types of people from different parts of the country and world and offer them hope. This hope grew out of my family's foundation and legacy of faith— both of which I am thankful for.

———•—

My family consisted of my dad and mom; my older brother, Chad; my younger sister, Holly; and me. We lived in a little

A-frame house on Mound Street. It was only two bedrooms. I shared a room with my brother, and when my younger sister was born, my dad and some friends opened up the attic for another bedroom.

During those childhood days, life was about riding our bikes to the creek, which was really just a ditch. There was a little playground at the end of our street. And for a real treat, we'd ride our bikes to the pharmacy where we'd get three or four scoops of ice cream for fifty cents.

My mom worked at a loan company that was near a video rental store, but Chad and I weren't allowed to cross the busy highway on our bikes to get to either place, though we tried a couple of times and got caught. My parents wanted us to wait for them to take us to the video store, where I'd usually rent my favorite movies, *Superman* and *The NeverEnding Story*.

My Granny Louise would come and pick us kids up in her white Ford Crown Victoria for Sunday-night or Wednesday-night church. If one of us came out with shorts on, she'd make us go back in and put pants on 'cause, you know, we were going to church. She always had friends she picked up along the way too—old ladies who smelled strong of flowers. Ladies who had little, but that didn't matter as long as they had Jesus. Even now I can remember the laugh of one widow, Sister Deshazier—it was like high little bells that would ring out through the car.

Back then, church seemed to be mostly about rules. Thinking about it now, though, I believe many of the rules came from the way I processed things, not necessarily what people told me. Growing up, I knew men wore long sleeves to church and women wore long dresses and didn't cut their hair. My Granny Louise and her friends were old guard, and around them things happened just so. Granny always sat on the front right side of the church, and I would sit with her every Sunday morning.

Every few weeks, it seemed, I'd be up front singing another special. The two songs I remember singing the most were "He Grew the Tree" and "God Likes People." If anyone ever grew tired of me singing those songs, they didn't let on.

I'd also sing with the other kids from Sunday school in a choir we called the Booster Band, maybe because we were all so tiny and needed to sit in booster seats. We'd sing, "Booster, Booster, be a Booster" to the tune of "The Battle Hymn of the Republic" lyrics, "glory, glory, hallelujah." And then we'd sing another song like "Climb, Climb Up Sunshine Mountain" before going back out to sit with our families.

There was never an official church choir. Instead, when worship started, Pastor Evans would welcome the choir to come up, and whoever wanted to join could. This basically meant a whole group of people moved from the pews to the front of the church, and I was right there in the middle of them. And even if our singing wasn't completely enjoyable, everyone nodded along and applauded at the end because worshipping the Lord was the important part.

People always stopped by to see Granny when they needed help. And she really cared for everyone—those she knew well and those she didn't. If a friend's friend had an aunt whose cousin got killed, we'd go by the funeral home to pay our respects because that's how you showed love in a community like that. And Granny prayed for them all. She'd pray throughout the day, talking to God as if he were right there with her. Thanking him for things big and small. Her acknowledgment of his goodness rolled off her lips as naturally as breathing. Sometimes I wondered if she even realized she did it.

I clearly remember walking into church with my Granny Louise and looking at the white cross in the top of the arch above the door. I was probably four years old, and we sat on slatted pews, my feet swinging back and forth. Pastor Evans was my pastor for all of my growing-up years, and he and his wife, Sister Evans, lived across the street from the church.

There are two things I remember most about Sister Evans. First, she wore her black hair all piled up on her head, like most church ladies did back then. Second, she made the best coconut cake. And the way the cake was all piled up reminded me of her hair.

My dad didn't go to church much in my early years. He worked in the paint and wall-covering industry as an interior designer. He started out learning about painting and wall coverings, but then he got to the place where he could take a project from the drywall to a fully designed and decorated room.

He continued in the interior design business until 1987, and then—as he tells it—in a revival, God got ahold of his heart. This is what happened to my parents. Dad and Mom both knew there was going to be a shift and change in the life of our family, including Dad's work. This revival renewed Dad's desire to go into ministry, something he'd pushed to the side as he became an adult.

My dad tells the story of feeling like God had called him into ministry when he was twelve years old, but instead he got married and found a job that could support his growing family. When we moved into Granny's house, Dad could hear her words coming through the air-conditioning duct as she prayed that her family would get right with God. And she saw those prayers answered.

Dad started his schooling to become a minister and soon left his business. He followed the call to preach that had stirred within him when he was younger. God moved quickly, and soon Dad was asked to preach at revivals all over the Southeast.

He did this as an evangelist first, going from church to church speaking. Almost every weekend I'd go with him. Chad played baseball and Holly was too young, but I'd travel with my dad, and when he was done preaching, I'd sing.

Some weekends I didn't want to go, but I wanted to please my dad more and wanted to do the right thing. And I also enjoyed time with my dad. I appreciated the smile he gave me when people asked me to sing.

As we drove, I heard stories of my dad's grandmother, whom he'd never met. Lily Tilghman had raised ten kids alone—my grandfather, Big Daddy, being the oldest—after her husband died. Lily had been a woman preacher in Mississippi during a time when women preachers weren't popular at all. She'd travel by buckboard wagon to preach and serve. At least Dad and I could go by car.

We would travel from small country church to small country church, parking our car out on the white gravel lot in front. We'd sit in the front pew side by side. The congregation would sing songs from the same red-back hymnal, which was always interesting to me since not all the hymn books were red; some were green. Often the preacher would get up and say, "What do you want to sing?" A member of the congregation would call out the number of the hymn, and they'd all sing that.

Dad would preach, and sometimes he'd sing. I'd sing, too,

handing my cassette-tape music to the person who took care of the sound. We'd stay over at the pastor's house, and after church we'd usually eat ham-and-cheese sandwiches and chips. Sometimes we'd be treated to Chinese food or Shoney's. Those were special days.

I remember once trying to start the truck for Dad, and I didn't know how a stick shift worked. I turned the key and the truck jumped forward into the back of another car. Thankfully church people are forgiving.

During the week I'd spend a lot of time with Granny while my mom and dad were at work. I can still remember her humming as she cooked. I started singing those hymns, too, around the house and as we drove down dirt roads, past fields and forests. Rarely a day passes when a hymn doesn't cross my lips. Even now I can hear the words of our choir director hollering out, "Turn to page three, three, three, 'I'll Fly Away.'"

Granny lived with us for the last three or four years of her life and worked as a seamstress to make money. Her sewing machine was music to me. The foot pedal would slow down and speed up to the cadence of the gospel songs on her lips.

I can still picture her laying out those thin, brown patterns and pinning them to the fabric. People would also bring her pants that needed to be hemmed and jackets to be taken out. It was how she made her money and also how she showed us kids her love. She made us outfits for holidays and costumes for school plays. Once Granny even sewed me a satin vampire's cape that was red on the inside and black on the outside. I can't help but smile thinking about that. Granny was full-on holiness; the fact that she sewed me a cape so I could be a vampire really shows a grandmother's love.

Just like Daddy took me along to evangelistic meetings to sing, Granny took me along to "minister" to her friends, which was her fancy way of saying that I'd go along and sing. Singing was both entertainment and spiritual encouragement to Granny's friends. I sang at nursing homes, church gatherings, and community events. I sang at women's conferences and at senior events in the church's fellowship hall. When I was nine, I won second place in a singing competition at the county fair.

In nursing homes, I'd follow Granny into the large common room where many of the residents would be gathered. I remember those rooms always smelled the same to me, like cafeteria lunch, probably because those common rooms were also where the meals were served.

Granny would talk to people and pray for them, and I'd follow along. Thin, frail hands would reach for me and take my hand in theirs. Even as a boy my heart would break as the elderly clung to me, asking me to stay and not wanting me to leave. They'd tell me that no one had come to see them, and my tears would come. Then Granny would ask me to sing, and I'd see smiles.

I remember the music of the church more than the preaching. Singing about hardships, people suffering, and the glory to come. For those two hours of church service, the saints in our congregation could forget all the troubles outside the doors. They sang about looking forward to heaven and finding hope there.

But as a kid, I didn't have the same joy in knowing "when the roll is called up yonder, I'll be there." Because I heard a lot about hell, I was afraid of it, and I knew I didn't want to go there. I constantly worried that I wasn't going to do things good enough to get into heaven. I believed I had to walk the line to make God happy. There were certain standards I believed I had to keep.

Those feelings of not getting it right or not being good enough for folks are things I still struggle with. I tend to focus on the things that make me feel inadequate.

When I was a little bit older, but still a child, some of the formalities in the church relaxed a bit. Sitting next to the older ladies with their bunned hair were younger ones with frosted tips. Granny still wore long dresses, but my mom wore a skirt and suit jacket. Another big change was having a projector set up front, displaying lyrics on the wall. That's when praise and worship songs came in. The Hosanna! Music praise songs were the ones I liked most.

My happy, routine life changed one day when a family member picked me up at school. Chad, Holly, and I normally would have been on the bus with our redheaded bus driver, Mrs. Boday. Since we lived in a small enough town, it seemed like Mrs. Boday was everyone's bus driver—no matter where they lived—and she always dropped us off right in our driveway.

Instead of riding the bus, Becky picked us up. Becky was technically my cousin, but she seemed more like an aunt to me. Chad, Holly, and I rode quietly to Becky's house, and I knew something bad had happened—I just didn't know what. When we got there, we sat around a little round breakfast table and waited. My dad was out of town, but after a few minutes my mom came in. Her eyes were red and puffy.

"Kids, I have something to tell you. Granny died today. She's gone."

"No, she's not," I blurted out. "I just saw her." My chin quivered, and it made no sense. She couldn't be gone. She couldn't.

I thought about the last week. Granny had been in the hospital because she'd had an aneurysm, but she'd been doing better.

My parents told us the doctors were just keeping her in the hospital for observation. We'd even gone to visit. As the days passed, I expected her to come home soon.

"The doctor said Granny was doing better," I added, still not believing this was possible. But from the sad look in my mom's eyes, I knew it was true. Over the next few days, all types of people came over to our house, bringing food and meat trays.

It was a hard blow losing Granny. Pastor Evans spoke at her funeral, and the church was filled with people from near and far. As a seamstress, she had known a lot of people who dropped by with items for her to sew or alter. Granny would offer them a chair and a cup of instant coffee. She'd pray with them too. Some people would call, and she'd pray with them over the phone. I'd often hear her praying for all their needs when she was alone in her room. But now she was gone.

When we got back to our house after the funeral, most of the church people followed us there. Where we live in the South, if someone passes away, all the cars converge at a family member's house. People bring food and stacks of casserole dishes.

I couldn't handle all the people, knowing the reason they were there. I ran outside and sat by a tree in the backyard. I just didn't want to believe that Granny was gone. I couldn't face it.

It's not like I hadn't dealt with death before. Once, I remember Granny and I had gone to pay our respects to the family of a little girl who'd been hit by a car. She'd had long, red braids, and everyone had been so sad. But this time it was different. It was someone I loved dearly who was gone.

I still didn't want it to be real, and I remember humming the tune of *The NeverEnding Story* theme song. Even then I couldn't stop the heartache.

When I was fourteen, we moved to Meridian, Mississippi, and that year I tried out for a local singing group called the Merrystreet Players. The audition was at the Grand Opera House in Meridian, but back then the building was in disrepair. At the audition, everyone just got onstage and sang a few lines a cappella, but I was prepared. I had a cassette tape to sing "Wind Beneath My Wings," which I had sung at weddings and other events. It wasn't a Christian song, but it was an inspiring one. I was drawn to songs like that. I laugh now, thinking back on how everyone had gotten up and sung a few lines a cappella but I went above and beyond and did a full production. It earned me a spot in the group, and we traveled to other schools in the area to perform.

As a teenager, I didn't think becoming a popular singer on non-Christian radio stations was a possibility. I wasn't in Hollywood or Nashville. I had a good voice, but I didn't have a pop-star type of personality. I was a chubby teen who sang in church and whom old ladies loved. I believed people expected me to do a certain thing with my music, and I did.

Brooke tells me that my role in my family was being the responsible kid. I wasn't one to make a fuss when asked to serve in church. People counted on me. And it's not like I didn't enjoy serving. Looking back, I can see that so much of my service as a pastor had its beginnings in my upbringing. I can't tell you the number of times I've sung at the bedside of the sick and the dying. When my heart is breaking to see someone hurting or in pain, the best thing I know to do is sing. Holding somebody's hand and singing a favorite song brings that person peace, even with a hard diagnosis or struggling breaths.

Around the time I auditioned for *The Voice*, I sang by the side of a dear saint from the church. I'd sing favorite hymns, and then she'd always ask me to sing "You're Nobody till Somebody Loves You," an old Dean Martin song from the 1940s. Her face would light up as I sang. I've realized over time that good songs stir emotion. There is a lot more music beyond hymns or Christian songs that can help people smile.

As I sat by this woman's side, she'd tell me about the flowers and the birds she saw as she peered into heaven, and then she'd share what she'd had for lunch. As she hovered between this world and the next, I wondered if my songs mixed with those of the angels—maybe they even sang along.

At age seventeen, I became the worship pastor at our church. It was while I led worship, even as a teen, that I felt most connected to God—most alive. The experience was different from singing for the Merrystreet Players. It was more than just carrying a tune or singing an uplifting song like "Wind Beneath My Wings." Leading worship was not about the audience or about my voice. I saw God working through me in ways that were beyond myself.

During my teen years, my parents and our church had started reaching out to those who were hurting, broken, and struggling with addictions. The congregation grew as it filled with people who felt they were at the end of their ropes and needed God desperately.

By eighteen, I was a youth leader too. And that's when things really started to change. I can't pinpoint when, but around this age singing became more than about the songs. I connected with God in the music, and I helped others do the same.

When my dad tells about those days, he gets choked up sharing how during the singing and worship time people would come to the front of the church for prayer, to repent of their sins, or to dedicate their lives to God. They didn't wait for the sermon or the altar call invitation to come up to the front. Instead, through the times when I led worship, God reached them, and they rushed to the front.

Music was an escape from the hard stuff of life for me too. I was starting in ministry, but I was still a teenage boy. I wanted to serve God. I knew then, as I know now, that we are called to live a righteous life. That means having morals and virtues. It means being honorable and following God's ways as best as we know how. So, as a teenager at school, I didn't feel I could hang out with friends a lot, because I knew I shouldn't do the things they were doing, like listening to certain music or watching certain movies. There were friends who had drinking parties, and I went to one or two of those. But over time, especially after I started leading worship at church, I really tried to stick to the straight and narrow. At times I felt isolated from my peers—not all of them, but a lot of them.

When I started dating Brooke, she also pushed the boundaries of what was deemed acceptable by the older crowd, like wearing pants to statewide church functions. Things like that would cause eyebrows to raise. And once, when she had sprayed glitter all over her hair—just being a teenager, just being funky—our friend told her that her hair needed to get saved. He was sort of joking, but sort of not. For a time, I even felt like I loved Brooke more than God, so I broke up with her.

After high school graduation, I started taking college classes and struggling with the work. It wasn't easy, and I didn't see how it would help my future—not when I had goals to serve God and work in the church.

Realizing I didn't want to do the college route, I started working on becoming ordained in the Church of God and became a pastoral intern within our church. That's when I started comparing myself to the older men of God I knew in ministry. They were dynamic preachers. Their messages were insightful and moving, while I felt my sermons were more plain and practical. These pastors and leaders also stood in front of the church in pressed pants and starched shirts. They were more dignified in their delivery and their dress, and I wished I could be like that. But it didn't fit who I was. When I first started leading worship, I wore a tie, but I was a khaki pants and button-up shirt type of guy. As I started being myself, the expectations of how I needed to dress eased up, both within church leadership and within myself.

Yet, through all these struggles and pressures, the comparisons and worries slipped away when I sang. Music was my special bond with an eternal God.

In the years I'd been our church's worship pastor, the lyrics weren't just ones I was repeating; they became my own. I could feel them deep down. The songs moved from my head and my lips to my heart and my soul. My feet started moving, too, not because it looked good onstage but because I couldn't *not move*. It didn't matter how I looked; the music bubbled up, and my feet bounced until it seemed like I was dancing six inches off the ground. Sometimes tears came as I sang. Other times laughter. The words were more than just words; they started to reflect my relationship with God.

While the world around me was still watermelon slices on the front porch, blackberries in a bucket, and breezes through the cottonwood trees, within the church walls a different breeze was blowing. It was God's Spirit.

Like leaves quivering in my gut, music became the way God's goodness plopped like sunshine rays in the center of my being. I wish Granny could have seen that—not only the boy who grinned as he sang in front of the church but also the man who couldn't stop smiling as he sang, even when life was hard.

———•—•———

When I look back at my childhood, I can see that God used me even during times when I felt I didn't measure up. This was true when I was on *The Voice* too. Every time I got a yes, I'd thought it was going to be a no. Every time. So the surprise and the joy were very real when I kept getting chosen, kept getting a yes.

When I look for the wins, I see that God's ability to use us is greater than our doubts. I've had so many people send me messages, telling me how my joy displayed on *The Voice* was exactly what they needed during the hard season of a worldwide pandemic, when so many familiar things—like going to school, work, and church—were stripped away. The good news is that this joy isn't something exclusive to me.

Maybe God's been following you through the cotton fields, the muddy waters, and the rhythm of trains on firefly nights like he did me. Or maybe he's been following you through skyscrapers, expansive bridges, and crowded sidewalks. Either way, consider how your childhood provided a foundation for your faith. Do you see any wins there?

For some of you, that foundation may be strong. For others, nonexistent. But from this moment things can be different. Whether you sing a song to God or just listen to one, consider music as a time to connect with him. Your Father is ready and willing to connect with your heart. Trust in his goodness and you just might find that joy bubbling up inside you too.

When we fail and fall short, it may be hard to worship and sing to God. Anything we try to earn or do will always leave us feeling unworthy. But thank God worship is not about our goodness; it's about his. Every note. Every song. And that is one great win we can all count on.

WINS FOR TODAY

✓ We win when we can look back at our childhoods and see glimpses of the unique talents and gifts that God gave us.

✓ We win when we thank God for the special people in our lives.

✓ We win when we notice how God's been with us through the years—through the good times and the hard ones.

✓ We win when we remember prayers answered over the years—our prayers and the prayers of others.

✓ We win when we slow down and use music as a way to connect with God. When we worship God, we lift our eyes off our problems and instead gaze at his goodness. We are reminded that God is with us, just as he's always been.

CHAPTER 2

Young and (Mostly) in Love

BROOKE

Daddy looked at me from across the dining room table, and I knew he still saw his little girl. But I hoped he also saw how much I loved Todd and how much I'd prayed to be his wife. I stood before Daddy, hands clasped behind my back, giving him the largest smile I could.

"I know the plan is to get married next year, but we're going to bump it up—to November. Maybe. Yes?" Once the words were out, I held my breath, waiting for the answer.

"Brooke, you've just graduated. You're only eighteen."

"I graduated last summer," I said, placing emphasis on the word *last*.

"And you know where you're going to live after you're married?"

My chin tipped up with determination. "Granny said we could stay in the apartment. It'll be just fine for us, at least to start."

"Of course, if that's what will make you happy." He reached across the table and took my hand, giving it a squeeze. "But we might need to look at that apartment. It could no doubt use a few coats of paint."

For as long as I could remember, my daddy rented out a house to Granny and an apartment over Granny's garage to a sweet lady, Elsie, well up in her years. Once I'd jokingly told Granny,

"Well, maybe if Elsie passes, Todd and I can live there after we get married." I totally didn't mean it, but Elsie was very old, and she did die, and the little place came open. The whole apartment was about as big as an average kitchen. It was tiny. But my biggest thought was of marrying Todd, of just us being together.

I felt so grown up as we set up our own place. There was a loveseat and a television. For the dining space there was a card table with two chairs where we could sit down for dinner.

The kitchen looked like it belonged in a dollhouse. You could walk across the whole length of it in two steps. Daddy had some leftover black paint, so we painted the cabinets black. Like everything else, Daddy got the paint dirt cheap, and there must have been something wrong with it because it spread like tar.

On the other side of the room, Todd and I put our bed—a hand-me-down from Granny. We painted the ceilings blue with clouds, just to brighten things up. And as I prepared for our wedding day, I thought about how this day almost didn't happen, mostly due to all the times we'd broken up. Or rather, I'd broken up with him.

The first time I met Todd, I was just an awkward thirteen-year-old. He was fifteen, and his parents started pastoring a church my family had attended several years back, which Daddy wanted to try going to again. That day at church, I talked to people I knew from before and didn't give any mind to the pastor's son . . . until he showed up at my house.

Friday nights around our house were pizza night. My older brother, Shaun, and older sister, Melanie, looked forward to it as much as I did. My dad was dirt cheap (did I mention that?), and we never went out to eat. But on Fridays, we splurged—or at least that's how it seemed back then.

My mom, dad, brother, sister, and I had gathered to eat when someone knocked on the front door. Daddy looked to Mama. "You expecting company?"

"No." She moved to look out the window. "It's the pastors from Cornerstone and two of their kids, coming for a visit."

Without hesitation, Daddy scooped up the pizza box and hid it in the oven, since there wasn't near enough to go around.

Mama welcomed in Pastor Tilghman, his wife, and their two teenage kids. I exchanged glances with Mama as they sat. Her gaze warned me that I better stick around. My brother and sister slipped out before Mama could give them the same eagle-eyed warning.

It seemed as if all the Tilghmans were talking at once and the noise level rose. Pastor Tilghman introduced his two kids that had come. Holly was a bit younger than me, and Todd a bit older, nearly sixteen. Their smiles were large, and they chatted as if we'd all been friends forever. They talked about the church, asked about our lives.

The Tilghmans stayed for a while, inviting us back to church on Sunday. Daddy promised we would be there. Before they left, Holly rushed up to me with a grin. "Want to come spend the night?"

We'd learned they lived the next street over, but since I didn't know Holly or her family well, I declined.

"Oh, I have to wash my hair." A lame excuse.

"You can wash it at my house, it's not a problem."

I hurriedly thought of other excuses until I figured my way out of going. The family left with joyful waves. We stood at the window watching as they walked back in the direction of their house.

"Well, they're nice enough." Mama waved and smiled back as Daddy retrieved our pizza. "I think we should start going back to Cornerstone."

We did go back, and soon Holly became my best friend. As the months passed, I found myself spending a lot of time at the Tilghman house. Todd started driving, and I turned fourteen. He gave me a lot of attention, which I liked—always kidding around with me.

I first started thinking differently about Todd when he asked if I wanted to go to the movies with him and Holly. I enjoyed our time together—until he sat by me and started eating from the popcorn bucket I held on my lap. That got on my nerves, and I told my mama so when I got home.

I didn't think I liked Todd in a romantic way until his old girlfriend came down for a visit. Suddenly, I wasn't the one who got all the attention anymore, and I missed it. I let Holly know I liked Todd, and I found out he liked me.

Around Christmas he got me a big teddy bear, and I got him a gift too. It was then I knew we were dating, but as the year went on and we turned fifteen and seventeen, it seemed we were broken up more often than we were together. I always liked being with Todd, but I usually broke up with him because I didn't want to limit my options, being so young. While I didn't think much of breaking up, Todd took it seriously. After one of the times I'd broken up with him, I remember he called me and asked if I was sure.

"Take me back before I have to tell my parents." His voice echoed through the phone pressed to my ear. "If I tell them we're really broken up, then it's for good."

That "for good" lasted a little while, until Todd got another girlfriend, and I realized I didn't like that one bit. So we got back together again, and in my mind it was for good. At least, I was mostly sure it was.

Around this time Todd was nearing eighteen, and he started feeling the desire to preach. I worried about being a pastor's wife—I didn't seem to fit the mold. I didn't sing. I would do funky things with my hair. I wore pants to church. No, I didn't fit the mold of a pastor's wife. Yet I knew I was growing to love Todd, which is why I was so crushed when *he* then broke up with me.

Tears filled my eyes as Todd told me he felt his focus was more on *me* than on God—so he'd decided it was best that we part ways. It didn't help that not long afterward, he started dating someone else. Still, I went to hear him preach his first sermon at the church, and I felt so proud listening.

I had always been the one to see "who else was out there," but suddenly I realized that he was the one. I did love Todd. I loved his friendship. I loved his playfulness. I loved when he led worship, and I loved when he preached. I also knew that the only way we'd get back together was if God spoke to his heart.

Todd was dating someone who fit the mold of the perfect pastor's wife, but I wouldn't give up praying. I'd walk the halls of my house praying that God would bring Todd back to me—that I could be his wife. Sometimes Mama joined me in praying too.

Yet the thing about prayer is that while we often pray to get God to act, answered prayer usually starts with a change within our own hearts first. I ended up going to a softball tournament with a guy I knew, and Todd was there with his girlfriend. Todd was still playful, but he seemed to be extra annoying, picking on me. When I got home that night, I realized that while I'd been so set on marrying Todd Tilghman, God maybe had other plans.

"I give it to you, God," I prayed. "If it's not Todd who I'm supposed to marry, then that's okay."

Finally, I was at peace, and soon God did bring Todd back to me. This time it *was* for good. I was just eighteen and Todd was twenty. We got married November 14, 1998.

We moved into that tiny apartment over my granny's garage, and we had our first Christmas there. Todd worked at the church, and I worked as a receptionist at a doctor's office. We lived there a year and then moved to a duplex.

Six months after our marriage, I discovered I was pregnant, and nine months later we welcomed our son Eagan. The first six months after his birth, I thought I had the perfect life. But soon things began to change. In a short amount of time, I'd gone from living at home to being married to then having a child. And suddenly my happily ever after seemed like a whole lot of work and a whole lot of missing out on fun.

In our duplex, you could hear everything—people blow-drying their hair and flushing the toilet—and it had floor heaters that we had to block off so our baby wouldn't burn himself. There was brown carpet in the kitchen that would get wet every time I opened the washing machine, which was also in the kitchen—and a possum problem. A big possum problem.

We came from humble beginnings, and as simple as our life was, there was nothing simple about being married. My emotions easily swayed me in marriage just as they had when we were dating. I only wish that staying in love was as easy as falling in love. After a few years had passed, I wanted out—out of marriage with Todd, out of the life we had created.

My sister was single at the time, and she'd often invite me out. This started when Eagan was about six months old. I enjoyed going out with her and her single friends. We'd go to dinner and just hang, but it made me realize that by getting married so young I'd missed out on the single life.

Sometimes Eagan would stay home with Todd, but many times my mama would watch him. My mama kept him a lot. Todd liked his home-alone time. He let me go out a lot because he wanted me to be happy, but he enjoyed the quiet too.

Also, there was a doctor at work I enjoyed flirting with—not that I wanted anything to happen there, but it reminded me that I was pretty and guys considered me attractive. The flirtation flattered my ego. It felt good. My romantic feelings for Todd faded, and I believed there was something more exciting out there for me.

I knew Todd loved me. In a way, he loved me too much. He spoiled me just as my parents had, since I was the youngest. When we got married, Todd did all the cooking, all the cleaning. When I wanted to go out to eat or buy something, he'd say it was fine, even if we didn't have money for that. He'd lie and tell me it wasn't a problem, but in truth he wasn't taking care of our other expenses.

Todd struggled with paying the bills. He'd tell me he'd paid stuff when he hadn't. Then I'd come home to find a note on our door saying we hadn't paid rent, and I'd get upset. So what did I do? I called his mama. "I'm gonna let your mama deal with you." That's how immature I was.

I used his struggle with money management as an excuse—and it did bother me—but my main motivation for leaving was because I had this fairy-tale dream that there was something better for me out there, someone better for sure. But even as part of me thought that, the other part of me knew it wasn't true.

I remember crying as I talked to my mom's pastor, "No one will ever love me as Todd loves me." I wanted to keep him as my best friend, but I was tired of being married.

There weren't many people I felt I could talk to. I'd grown up in church, and I'd started attending Cornerstone Church as a young teen. I'd married the pastor's son. The pastor's daughter—Todd's sister, Holly—was my best friend. Our lives revolved around the church. I was certain that if the church people we'd surrounded our lives with found out I was discontented and wanted to leave my marriage, they'd pick sides—and it wouldn't be mine.

Walls rose like tall fortifications around my heart. Todd tried to be sweet and loving, but those affections bounced off, not affecting me. The walls erected against the people at church too. Looking back, I wonder if they saw me retreating. I was polite but kept to myself. I moved from sitting in the front of the church to the back pew. This went on for months, until Eagan was nearly two. Even as Todd led worship up front, I'd tell myself that I could still go to church and be a Christian if I got a divorce—people did it all the time.

I never got the chance to date, I'd tell myself. *How do I really know that Todd's the one, since I have no one to compare our relationship to?*

I just wasn't satisfied. I pictured myself dating other guys and finding that exciting, romantic type of love I saw in movies. I wanted big emotions, not the steady, gentle commitment that Todd gave me. I fooled myself into believing that I could have an exhilarating new relationship and still have Todd as my best friend. Thinking about it now, it doesn't make much sense. But I was young and ignorant, and that's how my immature mind was thinking.

The question wasn't *if* I was going to leave my marriage but *when* I would have enough courage to do so.

TODD

I've been smitten with Brooke since the beginning. With those big blue eyes, her wide smile, and her passionate personality, she drew me in. Brooke is as adventurous as I am cautious. She pushes me to step beyond the safety lines I set around myself. Even though Brooke says she never felt like she fit the role of a pastor's wife, who says what that's supposed to look like? God obviously knew the type of wife I needed to help me get to where I am today.

Back in 1994 when we started dating, I'm sure God looked ahead and saw 2020 and 2025 and 2030. He knew that I would need somebody to push me like Brooke pushes me. I would have never stepped out to try a lot of things without her urging, including auditioning for *The Voice*.

I've always felt like Brooke was sort of out of my league. I was kind of a chubby teen when we started dating, and she has always been beautiful. With her magnetic personality, she's always had all these prospects, and at first, I didn't have any of those kinds of things going for me.

Let's just be honest, there are a lot of unwritten rules when it comes to dating, especially when you're young. I wasn't the guy that a beautiful, stunning young woman wanted to be with . . . until she did. And, after the many starts and stops to our relationship, I wanted things to stay that way. We pulled the trigger on marriage while we were too young and dumb to know how hard it could be.

On our wedding day I thought it would be special to surprise Brooke by singing to her. Back in those days all the songs were on cassette tracks, and an hour or two before the ceremony, I could not find my track. Panicking, I sent a friend to the Christian bookstore to buy another track. Before he even got back, I'd found the original track, and the singing went off without a hitch. I sang "Grow Old with Me," and I expected that was how things were going to be. Then, a few years into marriage, my world came crashing down.

In March 2002, we were (as far as I could figure) living an okay life. I mean, we were young and in ministry, and we had a child, so of course we were broke. Besides that, life seemed pretty good. Until one afternoon, when Brooke and I were sitting in the living room together in the midst of a quasi-argument. In my memory, the disagreement wasn't even that bad, until I heard the words coming out of Brooke's mouth: "I just think we married too young, and I don't want to be married anymore."

My mouth dropped open. I could tell by the firm set of her jaw and her narrow gaze that she was serious.

"I'm moving out, Todd. And nothing you can say is going to change my mind."

I urged her to give me a reason. Hadn't I done everything for her? We didn't have much, but I'd tried to do everything to make her happy. I ran a hand through my hair, attempting to make sense of this. "Is there someone else?"

She quickly shook her head. "There isn't anyone else, Todd. I haven't been unfaithful. I just don't want to be married anymore."

She doesn't want me. There's not someone else. She'd rather have nothing than me. I wasn't sure if knowing that made things better or worse. I jutted out my chin. "If that's your decision, then you're going to be the one to tell my parents."

A look of panic crossed Brooke's face, and then, just as quickly, it disappeared. Her eyes narrowed. She turned her back to me. "Okay, I'll tell them. I'm not going to change my mind."

Brooke's words caused me to suck in a sharp breath. *How can this be happening?* I knew we weren't as close as we should have been, but her decision was like a baseball bat to the chest. *Not enough . . . I'm not enough,* I thought to myself over and over again.

Brooke sat quietly next to me as we drove to my parents' house. I knew that telling them was probably going to be even harder than telling me. From the time we were first engaged, my parents worried that Brooke and I were too young. Also, she was indecisive about a lot of things. When we first got married, we both knew that they worried Brooke would change her mind, and now her decision was basically proving them right.

When we sat down with them, my parents didn't let Brooke off easy. They wanted to know her reasons for wanting a divorce, and she finally had to admit that she wasn't romantically attracted to me anymore. She said she loved me, but not in a romantic way. Nothing she could have said would have made me feel better, but somehow that made me feel worse.

The next day, Brooke left to move back with her parents, and I remember sitting and staring at the TV, which wasn't even on. My parents said they were going to come over, and I told them not to, but they still did. I was so furious with them.

Let me be alone.

I remember feeling really low. I felt fat and unwanted. I had gained weight, and even my parents had brought that up. Brooke telling my parents that she wasn't romantically attracted to me had hurt. Some really ugly things were said, and not just by Brooke.

Anger filled every part of me. I finally called the attorney. "How do you handle this if you don't want it to happen?" I asked. "The only paperwork I'm willing to sign is paperwork that says I don't want a divorce." I wanted to make our marriage work, but Brooke refused.

In the period that followed, we fought and complained about each other to anyone who'd listen. We made sneaky plans to keep our son away from each other. We met with people for advice, but their advice didn't seem to make a difference. Brooke was done.

For Brooke, once news spread that we were getting a divorce, there was no return. She had pulled off the Band-Aid. All the people whose reactions or responses she'd feared now knew. All the pious peering down the nose was underway. She had done the hard part.

For me, the hard part was owning my fault in this suffering. *I didn't do anything to deserve this*, I told myself. Yet, as the months passed, I discovered that *I* was part of the problem. I was right. I hadn't done *anything*—or at least not much of what I needed to be doing.

I hadn't been awake. I hadn't been vigilant in our marriage. It was easier to simply let Brooke have her way than to work with her to figure out what was best for her and our marriage.

I'd been asleep at the wheel of our marriage, or on cruise control at best. Wanting to make Brooke happy, I'd allowed her to go out with her single friends, until she decided that the single life was better and happiness wasn't found with me.

At that time, church was my world, but I felt like a hypocrite. I led worship, pointing others to Jesus, but my heart was split in two. I was the youth pastor, but what advice could I give to those teens?

Looking back, even though Brooke had been struggling with selfishness, I'd struggled—and still struggle—with pride. I wanted people to think our life was good and everything was okay. I wanted it to always seem as if we were doing everything right. And Brooke telling me she wanted a divorce shined a light on the troubles in our marriage.

Yet even being the pitiful, broken person I was, I also knew that if things were going to change, it had to start with me. I stopped fighting Brooke and entered into repentance, which basically meant that I told God I was sorry for my part. Instead of fighting her, I tried to just do my best in caring for her, even when she didn't appreciate it.

BROOKE

When we first got married, I didn't realize that love is a choice. I started to listen to the lies that the grass was greener "out there." I started listening to the wrong people. I wanted to be free.

Not long after Todd and I went to tell his parents, I met a lawyer who said he could work quickly, and he had the paperwork drawn up within a week. I was determined to get this part of my life over and done with. The biggest concern about the divorce was that we had our son.

The day I told Todd that I'd be moving out, he informed

me that I could go but I couldn't take our son. "You can leave, Brooke, but you're not taking Eagan. You're choosing to leave, but this is his home."

I know this seems horrible, but I knew if Todd had Eagan, then things would be easier on me. I could go out and live the single life and not have to worry about a babysitter.

I moved back in with my parents, and during the day, Todd dropped off Eagan with my mom since both Todd and I worked.

While my parents wished my marriage had succeeded, they also supported me. They wanted me to do what I thought would be best for me. But I knew that not everyone would be so understanding.

When Sunday rolled around, I didn't go to church. I didn't want to hear what anyone had to say. Divorce is discouraged in the church. Pastors preach about the sanctity of marriage, which means that marriage is holy and established by God. Church weddings emphasize that the vows are taken between you and your spouse, but also between you and God. I knew all my church friends would try to talk me out of the decision I'd already made. And sure enough, the phone started ringing, but I ignored it. I didn't want anyone to tell me I needed to go back to Todd.

A young mom and friend at church didn't stop bugging me until I agreed to talk to her. She was in a bad, abusive marriage. "Brooke, you're married to a man who loves God and loves you. You're trying to throw away the very thing I've been praying for. You're giving away this godly husband and marriage to chase something that might not be there. You're following feelings instead of looking at what you have." She reminded me of the things I needed to be grateful for.

After I'd moved out of our home for over a week, a surprise

visitor showed up at my work. My eyes widened when Todd's mom walked in. Even before she was my mother-in-law, she was the pastor's wife. My chest tightened, and I balled up my hands on my lap.

She approached the receptionist desk where I sat. "Brooke, I'd like to take you to lunch. I thought it would be nice for us to talk."

I chewed my bottom lip. That didn't seem nice to me. I'd made up my mind. I didn't want anyone to try to talk me out of it. But I also didn't feel I could say no. No one said no to Sister Tilghman. Maybe it's a southern respect thing, but I nodded my head, rose, grabbed my purse, and joined her.

She drove me to a Mexican restaurant, and even before the chips and salsa arrived, she looked tenderly toward me from across the table and offered a soft smile. I felt myself erecting that wall around my heart again, determined that I wouldn't let her words change my mind.

Sister Tilghman talked to me about commitment. She talked to me about romantic love, attraction, and other things that caused me to blush.

I nodded, but nothing she said had changed my decision. I glanced at my watch. "I really need to get going. I'm already late to get back."

Sister Tilghman nodded, but she didn't seem in a rush to leave. "Brooke, I'm not asking that you change your mind now." Tears rimmed her eyes. "I'm just asking that you give it six months."

I shrugged. "Yeah, I'll think about it," I told her, even though I had no intention of doing that.

I still knew that I wanted to leave. But as days passed, I was getting tired of the fight. There were all these people trying to give me advice about what to do with Eagan. There were so many people who wanted to call and encourage me, but the pressure from them was a lot. *Why were so many people fighting against what I wanted?* They weren't making things easy.

I didn't know it at the time, but that Sunday night, women at the church gathered to pray for me. What I did know was that the next morning, on Monday, when I called Todd to tell him that the divorce papers were going to be delivered, I couldn't go through with it. I'd called him at the church, and hearing his voice changed something within me. I called the lawyer back and told him not to deliver them after all. I still had no intention of staying married, but something inside caused me to pause.

I thought about what Sister Tilghman had said: *"Give it six months."* Maybe I was rushing things. Maybe I should go back home for six months just to get everyone off my back. That's what I decided to do in my heart. *I'll just come back for six months, but I'm going to leave again.* Of course, I didn't admit to everyone that last part.

Hearing that I was moving back in with Todd, Sister Tilghman and some of the other ladies went and completely cleaned our house, which was nice. Even though I was trying to push everyone away, they just kept caring for me the best they could.

I went back home with Todd, but my heart wasn't really in it. He slept on the couch, and I tried to keep at a distance. Once, when Todd and I were talking, Eagan came up and he put our hands together. Even though he wasn't yet two years old, he could sense that we needed to make things right.

Right after I moved back, we went out to dinner with Todd's family. Todd's brother, Chad, isn't a man of many words. Yet when we walked in together, Chad got up before anybody else, came straight over to me, and wrapped me up in a hug. Not only did Todd welcome me back but his family did too—even when I didn't deserve it. Especially when, in my mind, I wasn't coming back for good.

About a month after I'd returned home, some ladies from the church asked me to join them for their usual gathering. We were on the worship dance team, and we often got together to do Bible studies and encourage one another. I joined them against my better judgment.

We put on worship music and sang along. Then, they started praying for me, for my marriage. They didn't try to judge me or lecture me, but they did pray.

During that prayer time, I had a moment between me and God. I felt like I could either hold on to what I wanted and destroy myself or let it go and be free. In that moment, it was as if I could feel myself physically holding on to what I wanted. It was so freeing to let go and say, "I'm going to trust God to take care of my marriage."

When Todd picked me up that night from church, I turned to him and said, "Look, I don't know what's going to happen, but from tonight, I'm going to be different. I'm going to actually try."

There wasn't an overnight change inside of me. It wasn't like I woke up the next day and thought, *I'm so in love with my husband.* But, over time, I started to be thankful that I'd stayed. Brother Tilghman, Todd's dad, told us both that if we stuck it out and made it through, we'd come to a deeper love. I found that to be true. Ups and downs, heartbreaks and joys, more kids and miscarriages, work at the church, not having money, and everything else have caused us to work together and come together—and to have this deeper love. I've come to have such respect for Todd as a person. He is my best friend. When you choose to love somebody, that love magnifies.

Having a caring community, family, and church helped me stay when I wanted to run. "Give it six months" has turned into twenty more years.

TODD

When Brooke came back to our home, I had a huge wall around my heart. It was hard for me to believe that things were going to be okay. Even though there was never any infidelity, she'd wanted something else or someone else.

For me, I had to trust that things could be better. I had to trust God, even when I didn't trust Brooke or that things would work out in our marriage. What this looked like in practical ways was just doing my best not to obsess over what she was thinking, what she wanted to do, or what her intentions might be. I failed a lot, and I guess I succeeded some. I also tried to have conversations with Brooke about, moving forward, what was acceptable and what wasn't, like going out with single friends all the time.

Also, after she left, I had written scriptures and inspiring quotes on little scraps of paper. I posted them all over the house—on the mirror, over the kitchen sink, on the door leading outside, and in other places. For example, 2 Corinthians 10:5, which says, "We demolish arguments and every pretension that sets itself up against the knowledge of God, and we take captive every thought to make it obedient to Christ."

I needed my thoughts to be centered on faith, not fear. I

needed those reminders to give me hope. Later Brooke told me that after she started to try, and had decided to give our marriage a chance, those scriptures were encouraging.

I also kept leading worship. There were people who didn't understand how I could. They asked me how I was able to worship when so much in my life was falling apart.

I took time to really think about that. If you're struggling, if you're sad or depressed or worried, or if you've fallen into some weakness or sin, how do you get up and worship? I haven't ever heard an audible voice, but I do feel like the Spirit of God put in my heart one day that worshipping in spite of hardship is the whole point. If we worship only when things are good, do we really believe God is who he is?

During that season, almost every time I led worship, I would find some way to mention this. Don't let your worship be hindered by your life or what has happened, because your worship is not about you. You're not worshipping because you're worthy; you're worshipping because God's worthy.

I had to take things one day at a time, but really, that's all any of us can do. The change was slow. One day I went through the day and realized, *Wow, I didn't think about Brooke leaving today. I didn't obsess over that like I did before.* But every day that she stayed was a win, and over time our love drew us back together again.

It's been over two decades since this happened, but that time in our lives is kind of like dropping a glass in the kitchen. You think you've cleaned up all those tiny slivers of glass, but then one of those little shards draws blood. Even today, we can accidentally step on a tiny piece from that broken time, a little part we thought we'd cleaned up but didn't see. It's been hard work.

I don't have trust issues with Brooke, but I do have insecurity issues that may stem from that time. If it looks like she's been too flirty with someone, worries fill my mind. There have been other times when she's threatened to leave, and I've considered it too.

For a long while, whenever Brooke got mad at me, she'd post about it on social media. Here I was, working in ministry, and she'd post to all her Facebook friends what I'd done and why she was upset. Her anger would stir those old feelings within me of her being dissatisfied and wanting more than me.

Yet coming across a shard now and then is better than the alternative. If we hadn't stuck it out, there'd be no us, no seven more kids that we call ours, no albums of memories, and definitely no stepping out to follow my music dreams at my wife's insistence.

I think one of the more devastating aspects of our world is that when it gets to this breaking point, most people quit instead of seeing things through and finding out that life is so much better on the other side. For us, this breaking time was worth more than I can say. It taught us about each other, about God's grace, about restoration, and about how good marriage really can be.

Brooke and I also tell people that God often walks toward us in the storm. We get so frustrated and upset because the storm comes. We question why we're in a storm in life, but that's how Jesus came to his disciples too. In Matthew 14, the disciples were out in a boat when a storm came. They were scared of the rocky waters. Yet the rocky waters were the means by which Jesus got to them that day.

Brooke and I aren't perfect. We still fuss at each other, but we're committed. Sometimes I look at my family and think about what we could have missed, like when I'm sitting in the recliner at the house and our youngest child, Winnie, is fixing my hair. Moments like that would not exist at all. What we're living right now, well, it just seems like our destiny.

BROOKE

I wish I could say that after this incident I never struggled again. There have been times when I still believed the grass was greener on the other side. There have been hard times when I thought about leaving. But I discovered that feelings aren't everything; commitment is.

I am also thankful for God's work in our lives during that time. If we'd not had that storm—if God had not come to us in that way—I have a feeling we wouldn't still be married now. We had to walk through what we walked through to correct some things. We had to rebuild some of the foundations of our marriage that had been built wrong.

Like Todd preached before, we had to put God back at the foundation of our marriage. From his point of view as a husband, Todd needed to do his best to please God more than he tried to please me. And I had to put both God and Todd before myself. I had been very selfish and me-centered. And then we had to build our relationship with each other.

I know every relationship ebbs and flows. Your spouse is going to hurt you. You're going to hurt your spouse. But it's important not to let those hurts break what you have. Marriage is hard work, and you have to put in the effort.

When I first came back home, Todd dealt with his hurt heart

by being sarcastic. If there was something I wasn't happy about, he'd say things like, "Oh, that doesn't matter, she's just going to leave again." He'd joke about it in front of everybody, and it really hurt my feelings. I talked to him about saying those specific things, and he stopped doing it. But he still sometimes gets sarcastic to cover his hurt. We both know now that it's a defense mechanism, and we process through it together.

Also, I'm a confrontational person and Todd is not. If I can tell that someone is bothered by something, I want to deal with it. Todd is more passive. Sometimes when there were issues in church, he'd tell me, "Don't worry, it'll work itself out."

"Todd, it's not going to work itself out," I'd tell him. "You have to deal with it." He gets under my skin when he handles situations differently than I would handle them. He tells me, "It's not my place," and I tell him, "Well, someone's got to do something."

But that's who Todd is. I love him, I respect him, and I'm proud of him. Todd has always put me, his kids, and the church first. My personality is to be the center of attention, and I'm choosing to take a step back and allow Todd to take the role as the leader.

And that's what made it so special to cheer him on at *The Voice* and to continue to cheer him on as so many, many more people are excited about his music.

Marriage is a covenant—good days, bad days, ugly days. If your love is about you, that's not love at all. Even right now, with all the changes in Todd's growing music career, I want to love Todd well. That's what God has put on my heart.

———◆———

When I got married, I thought it was going to be this fairy-tale fantasy movie. When it wasn't, I wanted out. If you're at the place where you want to give up on your marriage, I understand. But, as my mother-in-law told me, "I'm just asking that you give it six months." Hang on. Don't quit. Keep going. Put one foot in front of the other. Those are all wins. And if six months seem like too much, ask yourself: *Can I make it five minutes?* I admit I had to start there too.

We also win by making time for each other. Now, every year near our anniversary, we go to the mountains for a week. We started doing that consistently for the last ten years. We were so poor for so many years, but after Todd took over as pastor, we'd often get a financial gift for pastor appreciation in October, and our anniversary comes after that. We go on small hikes. We watch movies. We sit in the hot tub and relax. We find places where they don't have great phone service, and we are able to leave the high-pressure situations of work or church behind.

It's our way of investing in each other, a way to reconnect. We engage in conversations that we don't normally have, whether they're about our intimacy goals, our family, or anything else we need to talk about without distractions. I love talking to Todd. He's so smart and funny. When I remind myself of those things, those are wins too.

We've learned to invest in smaller ways also. Sometimes I'll tag along when Todd goes on a work trip. Sometimes it's as simple as going to Walmart together, and then driving around the block so we can finish our conversation before coming home and being bombarded by kids.

We also use our strengths to help each other's weaknesses. Todd keeps me from just flying away in the fantasy land of whatever I'm dreaming about. But at the same time, I stretch him to do things. God put us together for that exact reason. Encouraging Todd's dreams led him to *The Voice*. I wouldn't let him *not try*. I didn't want him regretting and always wondering *what if?*

What I used to see as differences that pushed us apart, I now see as traits that God uses to help us balance each other out. Todd has always been my safe place. Whatever storm, whatever anxiety, he's always been there. We struggled when we were younger with really connecting on all levels. We have come a *long* way. And God taught us to love even when we didn't like each other very much. We have held on when many others would have quit.

TODD

Just last week, I met with two well-known songwriters, and we worked on a song that's been on my heart. The premise of the song is that you push the furniture back and make the living room your dance floor. You might not get to go out to the ballroom. Your kids might be down the hall going to bed in their rooms. But you can take this moment and make life out of it. The song is called "Living Room Dance Floor," and we'll be demoing it soon. I love it. Isn't that an amazing first song for me to have written with a professional songwriter?

Brooke and I don't always move furniture around, but we do dance around. And honestly, it's a good metaphor for marriage. There are times that I've made Brooke a steak dinner that we got to enjoy after the kids went to bed. We've learned not to wait for perfect moments but instead to make the most of the moments we have.

Marriage is about being loving even when you don't feel like it. It's finding special moments in the middle of ordinary days. It's putting the other person first when you don't feel like coming in second. All those are small wins, yet over time they culminate in big moments, like when I'm able to tell everyone on national television that I've been married twenty-one years to my wife, Brooke. Having her there with Eagan, cheering for me backstage, was a bigger win than anyone realized.

WINS FOR TODAY

- ✓ We win when we're willing to put the work into our marriages. You can overcome hard things together.
- ✓ We win when we realize love is a choice, not a feeling.
- ✓ We win when we show up for our spouses, even when we want our way.
- ✓ We win when we don't make rash decisions and instead realize that time *can* heal wounds.
- ✓ We win when we surround ourselves with people who will encourage our marriages and pray for us.
- ✓ We win when we turn to God for help, even when we don't feel like it and doubt anything can change.

✓ We win when we turn back during the times we think we've gone too far to ever go back. Even if you've made a bad decision, you can turn things back around.

✓ We win when we put ourselves second. The daily decisions we make to care for our spouses lead to big wins.

✓ We win when we see our differences as things that can help our marriages, not as things that can pull us apart.

✓ We win when we find special moments in the middle of ordinary days.

CHAPTER 3

Ministry Minded

TODD

When I was about six or seven, the congregation Granny was a part of built a new church on Carrollton Road in our town of Grenada. Up until a recent remodel, the pews they had were the same ones that I used to lay under. When the preaching would go on too long, I'd open up the tiny offering envelope and draw. That wouldn't make the deacons all too happy, of course. Those envelopes cost money.

Still, under those pews I heard stories about Jesus, and during the week, I learned about the faithfulness of the church people toward one another. Yes, they might whisper a "bless her heart" every now and then if something you did got their goose, but if you needed a meal or a helping hand, you were sure to get it. And your needs would be carried down the prayer chain, which is a fancy way of saying people would call one another up day or night to share a need and ask for prayer.

Looking back, I grew up thinking the church was my whole world. Most of the people I knew were church people because my life was so immersed in it. I didn't think of doing anything outside of church. No grand career plans loomed in my horizon, even as a teen.

Leading worship at sixteen seemed as natural as the warm welcome from the greeters at the beginning of church service and the firm handshakes on the way out the door. Church wasn't just a part of my life; it was part of everything.

When I sang and worshipped, it was as if everything else faded, disconnected, became unplugged. All the worries and concerns of the moment—from who I should date to whether I should keep going to college or drop out—faded. Instead I plugged into God. I felt the connection. New life flowed in as my soul connected with the words belting out from my mouth. Emotion flowed, as powerful as the Mississippi River, sweeping me away. If church was my familiar place, singing onstage was home. After I married Brooke, I sometimes worked other side jobs, but I was always working for the church from the time I was eighteen.

I grew up in a state where music was revered. If you come to Mississippi, the highway signs say it all: WELCOME TO MISSISSIPPI: BIRTHPLACE OF AMERICA'S MUSIC. The blues originated on the Mississippi Delta. Jimmie Rodgers, born here in Meridian, was known as the father of country music. B.B. King, Jimmy Buffett, and even Elvis came from Mississippi. But I never dreamed or aspired to take my music beyond the church crowd.

I found my own voice as I sang hymns written in ages past. And the newer praise and worship music gave me comfort in the inspiring phrasing. Songs like "Blessed Be the Name of the Lord" or "Our God Is an Awesome God" connected with my soul. And as I read God's Word more and more, I found myself wanting to share messages of hope with others, just like I saw my daddy do every Sunday. I started preaching to the youth at church. Even though I was still their age, I wanted to lead them—not because I wanted the responsibility but because I was serious about my relationship with God, and I wanted them to see how he could change everything in their lives too.

The desire to preach to an older crowd—adults, not just the teens in our youth group—first came at Camp Meeting, which is a state conference for all the churches within the Church of God. There's a Bible speaker in the morning and preaching at night. It's a time when pastors and their families get a chance to be served. It's also when the people who raised the most money for missions receive recognition, as well as graduates who went through the internship program. And there's always a women's banquet.

One night at Camp Meeting, the preacher asked everyone who felt like they were called to go into youth ministry to come to the front and receive prayer, so I did. While I was praying, something stirred inside me. I didn't hear God in an audible voice, but there was a sense in my soul, as though God was putting his finger on me and saying, *The anointing that you have isn't just for young people—for youths. It's for all types of people.* I didn't understand what that meant.

I knew that God had plans for me beyond youth ministry, but I also was opposed to being a pastor. I didn't feel qualified to be a lead pastor. I had grown up in a pastor's home for a lot of my life, and it seemed like more than I could handle—all the needs, all the responsibilities.

But then things began to change. I don't remember the exact point. Over time I felt God was moving me, shifting me in a new direction. In my midthirties I knew that lead pastoring was something I was supposed to do. I felt a stirring to reach people with love and hope—within the walls of the church and in our community.

BROOKE

The transitions of Todd moving from worship pastor to youth pastor and then to lead pastor happened gradually. Todd slowly took over more of the preaching, and his father became more and more involved in serving those who struggled with addictions. Both Todd and I wondered if that calling would take Brother Tilghman away from pastoring our church. We weren't worried about it, though. We had set our hearts to simply being open to whatever God had in store.

When Todd first accepted the role of associate pastor, he preached almost every Sunday night. By this time our family had grown. We had added two more sons: Asher and Shepard joined Eagan. At the time, Todd and I thought our family might be complete, and I loved how we were able to serve in the church even as we raised our three sons.

But soon we added our two girls to our family through adoption, and Todd felt a call to become a lead pastor—even if that didn't mean staying at Cornerstone. As we approached thirteen years of marriage, we talked to the bishop about trying out churches. We visited three or four different ones, and while we appreciated each of them, none of them seemed quite like home. None of them had our hearts like Cornerstone. But then one church asked us to come and be their full-time pastor. We asked them for time to pray before giving them a decision.

As we were worshipping at Cornerstone the next Sunday, I had a clear feeling that it wasn't time to leave. The service moved me, and I felt drawn to go up to the front of the church and speak to the congregation. "It's time for a shift," I said. "God

is going to do something. He's about to make a shift among us."
I didn't know at the time how much that shift would include me
and Todd.

As we settled into our vehicle that day after church—with
our five kids buckled in the back—I turned to Todd and told
him, "In church today, I just got this feeling. It's not time for us
to leave yet. We don't need to leave these people, Todd. These
are our people. We're gonna have to tell that other church no."

We'd told the other church we'd give them an answer the
next day. Todd looked at me with a cocked eyebrow, and I could
tell what he was thinking. I could see in his gaze he agreed, but
were we serious about saying no?

Out of the corner of my eye, I saw someone approaching. It
was Brother Tilghman. I rolled down the window and he leaned
in. "Don't take that other church," he said. "Your place is here.
God is moving me. There's a new and different ministry. I believe
you're supposed to stay here, son, and take over this church as
the lead pastor."

Todd and I looked at each other, and I saw a mix of surprise
and joy in his eyes. This was it. In a minute's time, a decision
had been impressed on us—and confirmed. My stomach flipped
and warmth filled my chest. I knew it had been God speaking
to me, to us.

Of course, the decision wasn't just up to us. The council, the
bishop, and the church had to vote. Everyone decided in favor
of Todd taking over as lead pastor, but the transition wasn't as
easy as you'd expect. His father had been the pastor since 1992,
and this was 2011. Brother Tilghman had grown that church
and had led the people well. Todd had big shoes to fill. Also,
Todd was very different from his dad. My father-in-law was from

a different era. Todd was more relaxed. Some people left the church because they preferred my father-in-law's style. It took a long time for people to even call my husband Pastor Todd.

Still, there were wonderful wins too. Todd always told those in our congregation that he didn't want people to feel they had to "clean up" to join us. He wanted us to approach people just as Jesus did, loving them just as they were and introducing them to the God who could make all the difference in transforming them into who he designed them to be.

TODD

If you visit Cornerstone Church today, you won't get two steps within the front door before someone greets you. And you may be surprised that as soon as praise and worship starts, most people find their way to the altar in the front to sing. They'd line up just feet away from the wooden stage that creaks a little as the musicians and singers play and move around.

The stage especially creaked and moaned every time I led worship, when the joy would overwhelm me and I'd find myself jumping as I sang—my holy hop.

I did most of my preaching at Cornerstone, but I've had the chance to preach at lots of other places too. No matter the size of the congregation, the setting, or the color of the skin of those within the pews, my goal has always been to teach and encourage. I wanted everyone to understand God better and see that he's not as distant or standoffish as they might have thought. No matter how they grew up thinking church people needed to be, I wanted them to know that they didn't need to clean up for God to accept them. Yes, changes may come later, but the heart of God is, "Come as you are."

I grew up with saints who wore dresses and suits and who found themselves at church three times a week, and I love those people. But we don't have to be that—none of us do. We don't have to clean up or get a new wardrobe to go to church or meet with God. Instead, we simply have to come as we are, me included.

My dad was still in the area when we took over the church in 2011, and one difficult part of the transition was that folks still looked to him. I'd go to the hospital to visit a church member, and as I entered, someone would say, "Pastor was just here." My dad had been to visit already, and it made me feel as if my congregants didn't really need me in a pastor's role.

I'd smile and nod, of course, but it took a while for everyone to see me as the pastor. For a bit of time, a lot of people continued to turn to my father for advice. Or when they didn't like what I was doing, they'd go to him about it.

But that dynamic wasn't the hardest part. Suddenly, all the problems of the church became my problems. Financial issues had caused the church to cut positions, which led to a church split and fractured emotions among those who stayed. There was no such thing as good feelings after church business meetings had gone bad, and the church stayed in that place for a while.

I made changes in my first few years as a pastor, and some church members had a hard time with them. Even something that seemed as straightforward as starting a missions program made some people mad at me. Yet their hearts started to change as they realized good things could happen when we served our community and even places beyond our community.

Things became more complicated when Cornerstone was taken to court. Even though the church was able to resolve the suit, the stress strained relationships. Dedicated members, whom Brooke and I considered to be like family, left the church. One blow after another struck my heart. Every day—for a long, long while—Brooke and I just waited for the next shoe to drop. We didn't wonder *if* another bad thing was going to happen—we wondered *when*.

Then all the bad things turned to the worst thing imaginable when we discovered a trusted church member had hurt one of our children. The story is our child's to tell someday, but it was then that Brooke and I wondered if ministry was worth it.

When the truth came out that our child had been hurt, I became really ashamed of myself as a father and as a church leader. I felt I should have known. Trying to process our child's pain and dealing with the offender was overwhelming. It was hard to even do day-to-day stuff.

It's hard enough to extend trust to people, but this really took away my trust in general. If someone this close to us could hurt our family, were there others who would do the same? People tried to pray for our family, but both Brooke and I felt numb. We often pushed away those who tried to encourage or help us.

During this season, we felt like we were doing what God had asked us to do. "God, how could you let us down?" we asked. We had to process that too.

When we tried to get justice, doors slammed in our faces. That's when God gave Brooke this scripture: "Do not take revenge, my dear friends, but leave room for God's wrath, for it is written: 'It is mine to avenge; I will repay,' says the Lord," (Rom. 12:19). Knowing that, we were able to start healing.

We took a month sabbatical from ministry. Brooke and I almost wanted to give up, but I had this inner feeling that when the time came for me to move on, I wasn't going to move on in failure and defeat.

In those dark days, we only had God to cling to. We had to trust that God saw our tears. And we had to learn to keep loving people, even when we wanted to push everyone away and seal up our hearts for good.

There were a lot of times when the role of a pastor was just too much. I've walked into hospital waiting rooms with families who have just lost their loved ones. I've had church members act out against me and others in the church. I've been called for advice and support after a suicide or the discovery of an affair. What do you say during times like that? I did the best I could, but I never felt I had all the right words. There are times when you have to be gentle and other times when you have to stand up and be strong to protect those in your congregation.

———•———

The good was mixed in, even with the bad. After one funeral of someone who died too young, another young man wanted to talk to me. He came to saving faith that day, which was a true gift, because not five days later he was killed in an accident. That's the good sandwiched between the hard, and to tell the truth, I found it challenging to come up with something to say over the caskets of twenty-year-old young men. Still, I offered what I knew, and that is truth, love, and hope.

Many parts of pastoring were good. We got to see people's babies born. We got to be with them when they were married.

We saw people freed from addictions and the chains of sin that plagued them for so long. We saw people restored in their marriages and learn to forgive those who hurt them. Both Brooke and I had the opportunity to share truth and hope in people's lives and be a part of God's good work.

One year we felt moved to do a program called "Take the Land," and we were able to lead the church in paying down hundreds of thousands of dollars of debt. We did not have a rich church, yet we were able to cast a vision. We owed a lot of money on our land, and now the debt was almost gone.

For every season, God puts pastors in place for a reason. In my season, our church took mission trips into the world for the first time. We started a ministry to the homeless and to the hungry. We got involved with the local pregnancy care center. It was beautiful to see our church start a Christmas ministry too. Our small church served our community in beautiful ways, and it was a big win.

As a pastor, you don't do these things on your own, but you do put your heart out there. Those who catch that heart, catch the vision, allow you to move in that direction and do those things.

For every flaming dart a pastor takes, there's at least as much fulfillment and reward. I know God called me to pastor, and I did. And for the last few years I also knew that my time of pastoring was coming to a close.

A couple of years before *The Voice*, I had an inner knowing that something was going to change, but I had no idea what or how. I wasn't discontented as much as I was unsettled. I felt at the end of my resources as a pastoral leader. I couldn't sleep at night. I'd wake up with anxiety.

I didn't know how to make a living other than pastoring. What could I do? How could I feed our big family? After we adopted the girls, Brooke and I had three more kids—Hosea, Louie, and Winnie—bringing the total to eight. The youngest is now four, and our kids span from ages four to twenty. That's a lot of mouths to feed.

We were in a very hard season. In an effort to figure out how to make money, I thought about real estate or even barbering. I could sing to those sitting in my chair, right? But even as I thought about those things, I also just kept loving the people God gave me to love in the moment. I spent my days with the family or in the church office or running around to the hospitals or showing up at people's wedding rehearsals or preaching at funerals.

Once I was asked to preach at the funeral of a woman I didn't know. I always want to be there for people, so I agreed. Before the funeral I spoke with the family. I asked them to tell me about this woman. During the sermon, I shared relatable stories about my own life. I wanted those in attendance to be able to walk away from that funeral knowing the love of God and how he could impact their lives.

After the funeral, one of the family members came up to me and said, "Next time you do someone's funeral, you might want to remember it's about them and not you." That absolutely crushed me. I tried to do the best I could to give a funeral for someone I didn't know, and in his eyes I'd failed. After that I often worried whenever I told a personal story that people would think I was full of myself. But I continued to love people and serve them the best I could, even if I didn't always get it right.

I can't count the number of hours I spent singing to people in their last days, bringing them comfort, just as Granny taught me. But Granny also taught me to have faith and to believe in big things. And daring to do both is leading Brooke and me to where we're going next. Brooke and I have now left full-time ministry at Cornerstone Church, and I'm following the many doors in music and singing that have opened for me.

Granny would have been amazed to see me singing on national television in front of millions of people. She would have been astonished that people paid to hear me sing in 2020, through live shows in Pigeon Forge and in other concert venues. God has opened these amazing doors, and I believe walking through them—taking my music and hope to the world—is the next chapter.

Looking back at that time of discontent a few years ago, I one hundred percent believe God was doing something in my heart to shift me into what he had planned next. As a whole, the church was good to me. I believe that discontent was God trying to move me into this new musical arena. He showed me that what Brooke and I saw in front of us was not the whole story. God sees the whole story, and he knew what was coming. Emotionally and mentally, he was setting me up for what was next.

BROOKE

Todd was very unique as a pastor. He's just who he is. He would confess where he'd messed up during every sermon. He's never one to act like something he isn't or to put on a show. Yet Todd also feels things deeply, and he always feels like he's not doing enough. Thankfully, God has reminded Todd that what he does to serve God and others is enough.

Once when we were in church, someone was praying with Todd and told him not to be discouraged. With a smile, the man told Todd that there would be a season when Todd felt like he was behind everyone else and should have made different choices, yet God would slingshot him ahead. We had no idea what that meant, but it did give us something to cling to. And looking back, we can see the truth of it.

Todd is ordained in ministry, but he has no college degree. We owned a house once, and only for a short time. Up until recently, we've had no savings account. Lots of people our ages were saving up for retirement, and we were still wondering if we could stretch the cornflakes and rice and beans a bit further. When it came to music, Todd never had any vocal training, and he'd never been on the road touring, but none of that mattered to God, did it? God took this opportunity with *The Voice* and has taken Todd into arenas we never could have imagined.

We've learned that we can look to God and do our best, but still not everyone will agree with our choices. And now that Todd's audience has grown and expanded, we understand there are some voices we need to listen to and others we don't.

We're still in the middle of God's story, even though *The Voice* may have brought a few chapter turns. God knew what was to come, and he knew what we needed to prepare for what was in store.

I also know that God knows Todd. Because of Todd's personality, he will always fall back on the safe bet. When Todd felt certain that his time as pastor at Cornerstone was ending after *The Voice*, he had to set a date to leave. We both knew that even though God had opened so many amazing doors with music, Todd's fear would overwhelm him, and it would be easy for him to fall back on the safe side if we didn't make concrete plans.

I feel that God knew that Todd needed something like *The Voice* to propel him beyond pastoring. Like Todd says, "God loved me enough to give me the grand gesture that he knew I needed." And God was so good to work in my life too.

When we started pastoring, I also felt very inadequate. But I felt God speaking to my heart: *You have to be who you are. You can't be like these sweet older saints.*

I never wanted to be fake, especially when Todd did something I was mad about. But I also had to learn maturity. I had to learn to know what to say when, and also when to keep my mouth shut.

Since I'm not administratively gifted, I had to bring people around me who were—like my friend Angela and my sister-in-law, Holly. I placed those people with me on my ladies' ministry board. I was able to use my gifts of having fun and making people comfortable, and they took care of the details. I was able to share what I felt God was putting on my heart, and I prayed with people.

Also, when Todd was gone during *The Voice*—and later during the transition—God matured me even more. When I knew we were leaving Cornerstone, I wanted to pull away to protect myself, but I felt God speaking to my heart: *Brooke, this isn't your church or the next person's church. This is* my *church.* I knew that until my assignment was up, God needed me there.

When Todd was gone in Pigeon Forge performing, I stepped up in his place and found myself spiritually guiding the services. I felt myself come full circle. People even told me that when it came to speaking or preaching in front of the church, I'd matured. By the end of our time as pastors, I'd become the pastor's wife I never felt I could be. It was bittersweet, but I felt God's approval as I knew our assignment was done.

Todd and I learned to be authentic in our church, but in a mature way. This has allowed us to be authentic no matter where we are. I believe that's why people fell in love with Todd on *The Voice*. He wasn't there to put on a flashy show. Todd just sang from his heart, and he shared a bit of hope along with it—just like he'd been doing for a while in our church home.

When Todd walked onto *The Voice* stage, we didn't think he would win. I know that Todd's voice is amazing; I hear him singing all the time. Yet, when he went onstage, we were just hoping he would get one chair turn so he could be on the show. But Todd kept getting yeses, and God kept opening doors. Todd's natural love for people was the platform that God used to reach the people in Meridian, Mississippi, for a long time, and suddenly it was the platform that God used to reach the world. Yes, people love Todd's voice, but I know they love his tender heart just as much.

When *The Voice* came home because of COVID-19, production sent tons of high-tech equipment to our front door. The intention was for us to film in our house, but as Todd told them, "We have eight kids in here, and one of them is feral. He'll be hanging all over the equipment." Thankfully, we had the ability to set it up at the church.

Our family and church friends helped set everything up in the craziness of national television broadcasting, and then Todd had to sing. He did his part, but the church people fed us. They hung lights. They kept our kids. They rejoiced with us and prayed. And they celebrated. God not only gave Todd this opportunity, but he also allowed our whole church to participate.

Tears filled my eyes as I watched Todd perform for a national audience of millions on the very stage where he first led worship and preached. On the very stage where we said our wedding vows. On the very stage where we've dedicated our children and shared the struggles of life.

Just like with our church family, people needed hope, and God was gracious enough to let us be a part of that. Recently, I was interviewed on a talk show called *Good Things*, and the host, Rebecca Turner, made a good observation: "I think America needed—they needed—a pastor, and they didn't know it. And even for the ones who maybe didn't care about his faith or the fact that he was a pastor, I think they liked him even because of that, even if they didn't know that's why they needed him."[1]

Todd's fear, my fear, of not being good enough for ministry has turned into freedom and joy. In the months ahead, Todd and I are looking to share God in new ways, and we can't wait to see what he has in store. Todd is phenomenally funny and loyal. He is authentic. He draws people in. From that stage he led a church, and from that stage he won *The Voice*. Only God could orchestrate something like that. And only God knows what is to come. Whatever it is, we trust him in that.

TODD

As pastors, there is no greater win than to see God work in people's lives and to be a part of that. There are no better relationships than church relationships. You can build a beautiful family through the church.

Also, a win is when people can come to you as they are. They don't feel they have to clean up or change. Love is a verb. It's a win when we focus on how to give love more than how to receive it. It's easy for us to say that we love the world, but people want to see it.

It was a win when I became known as the person the community could go to when people who wanted to get married needed someone to marry them, or when I became someone who could do people's funerals when they didn't have their own pastor to do so.

I work really hard to be Todd and let God be God. I can't change people, only God can. It's our job to just love them. And then, when you see people step out and help others—when you see the vision you reproduced in other people—that's a win.

WINS FOR TODAY

- ✓ We win when we understand that we don't have to be fully equipped to be called into ministry. God will equip us along the way.
- ✓ We win when we use our strengths and trust God to bring others to help where we are weak.
- ✓ We win when love is a verb. People need to feel our love before they understand God's love.
- ✓ We win when we show up.
- ✓ We win when we trust God. He always has more in store for us than we think.

CHAPTER 4

Bringing Our Girls Home

BROOKE

There are some people who say that they always knew they wanted to adopt, but for me it was more like spring in the South. One day you're driving and there's this chill in the air and everything's a dirty gray, and the next day you look around and everything's green with new flower buds popping up where there seemingly was nothing before. Adoption grew in my heart like that.

Before we married, Todd said he wanted two kids. I said I wanted three. So now we joke that we compromised on eight. I remember praying one day, and God promised me a little girl—I wanted a little girl so bad. We had three boys in a row, and maybe God was using my desire to stir something within. I love my boys. I love their energy, creativity, and laughter that always fill our home. But you know here in the South those ruffled pants and big bows are a thing. There was something about having a little girl to do those sweet things with. And then I heard about little girls overseas who needed homes through Steven Curtis Chapman's ministry, Show Hope, and that caused a twinge in my heart. When my mama-desire met a legitimate need, I felt this was something not just for other families out there, but for us.

Inspirational singer Steven Curtis Chapman and his wife have adopted three children, and I learned a lot about adoption through their ministry. My husband wasn't a famous singer, and we didn't have a lot of money, but I started reading blogs about real, everyday people who were adopting, and it inspired me.

The desire was building in my heart for a while, and when I have big things I want to talk about with Todd, I send an email— maybe to just get out all my thoughts at once. So I sent Todd a long email about adoption and my heart for it. He told me that when he saw he'd gotten an email from me, it alarmed him. He was driving, and he pulled over to read it. He agreed this was something we should look into. We believe God cares for orphans and that we could extend love to another child by bringing one into our home.

We originally looked into adopting from China, but we weren't quite old enough to adopt from there since China requires parents to be at least thirty years old. I'm impatient when God puts something on my mind, so I started looking into other places. We looked into the special needs program in South Korea, and we told ourselves we'd walk through every door that opened. But just starting that process took a lot of faith.

We thought the adoption agency would turn us down because we were youth pastors who already had three young boys, and we were broke. Actually, we were dirt poor. But every step we went through, they had a solution. "You can get a cosigner. You can do this. You can do that."

The agency told us it would be eighteen months to get a referral that would match us with a child, but we received one in four months. The email included a photo of Judah, and seeing her face for the first time was as wonderful as seeing the faces of my boys. She was beautiful, and she was ours. More than anything, I wanted her home as soon as possible. That's when everyone rallied around us to fundraise: our church, our family, our friends.

We had a yard sale, and everyone from our church donated nice stuff. We did a Biggest Loser fundraiser where people from church got sponsors for every pound they lost. We had a local restaurant give us 10 percent of the proceeds from their sales one night, and we invited everyone there. We did an offering at our church, and my daddy offered to match whatever came in. We picked up pecans at my parents' house and sold them.

We had a GoFundMe page. We made and sold T-shirts. We had a bake sale in front of Walmart on a freezing cold night. Lots of people just gave, especially during income tax time. We did a car wash, and I even went back to work for a time. We had a spaghetti lunch after church one Sunday, and the church never got tired of helping us. Then, the day before we were to turn in all the money, we were two hundred dollars short. Without knowing it, someone went to our GoFundMe page and gave two hundred dollars that very night. The time and effort to raise money for the adoption process wouldn't have been possible without everyone pitching in.

TODD

I had so many fears about the adoption. First, about finances. What if we couldn't get the money? It's quite expensive to adopt a child from another country. But when I saw the photo of Judah, I remember thinking: *This is my daughter, and I cannot afford to bring her home.* That was devastating for a person who deals with feelings of inadequacy.

The emotional cost was even higher than the financial expense, especially when the time grew closer for us to go get our baby girl. Even though we had approval, it took a while for the Korean government to get our travel paperwork in order.

We were hoping and praying that Judah would be home for Christmas, and she came home in February, which doesn't seem like a long time unless you're waiting with anticipation each day. Even when I was frustrated or emotionally broken down, I tried my best to make sure Brooke stayed even-keeled. When she'd be in tears about another day passing without news of when we could go get our daughter, I tried to be the voice of comfort and peace, even though I felt exactly the same way. I couldn't contain my joy when we finally got the travel call. *Finally. We finally get to meet our baby girl.*

We were two country folks who didn't know much about traveling when we went. I was also 310 pounds at the time, and because Brooke didn't want to sit by a stranger, I had to squeeze into a middle seat for fifteen hours. I'd go to the bathroom just to stretch my legs.

Then we had to figure out South Korea. We didn't speak the language. We spent a ton of money on taxi cabs. And, of course, the elephant in the room was that we were nervous about meeting our daughter for the first time face-to-face, and neither of us wanted to let on just how anxious we felt.

Landing in South Korea was both great and overwhelming. We were used to seeing Western Sizzlins, IHOPs, and Walmarts up and down the streets in Mississippi. But in Seoul, we discovered ancient traditions mixed in with a high-energy city. One street had designer boutiques and the next had a beautiful Buddhist temple. There were endless streets of food markets, and everyone was talking in this singsong way and we didn't understand a word of it.

When we got there, it was just me and Brooke for a couple of days. I told her right off that we were going to eat at a full-on Korean restaurant. I didn't want to go to a Burger King just because it was easy. So we found a restaurant and ordered all this strange food we didn't know what to do with. But it was delicious.

I was prepared from the beginning that our daughter might not like either of us right off. Judah was almost a year old, and she'd been with a foster family this whole time. Still, that didn't change my love or my excitement about meeting her.

We were on the street walking toward the building where we were to meet her, and we saw Judah's foster mom drive up in a car with Judah. After they settled into a room, we were brought in.

As we walked into the room, I remembered a dream I had when I was twenty years old. In my dream, Brooke and I had a baby girl with black hair. God had planted that dream in my heart, and now here she was. Our little girl was sitting on her foster mom's lap in the corner of the room, wearing this pink, really fluffy winter jacket. And she didn't want anything to do with us.

The translator asked us if we had any questions for the foster mom. We asked if Judah liked playing with other kids. We asked about her favorite foods. We also asked if she liked the music we sent her, because I had sent over a CD with my singing. Then we exchanged gifts with the foster mom.

We tried to approach Judah and hold her, but she started crying and clinging to her foster mom. She took it so hard that we didn't take her at that time. We set up another meeting, and we were able to take her with us then.

There were so many emotions going through me seeing Judah

for the first time. Immediate love for my daughter, joy at finally having her in my arms, and worry piled on with the happiness.

While we were there, we met a Korean woman who'd been adopted and raised outside of Korea but returned to care for orphans—reflecting the heart of God. I wondered, *Will Judah come back here, too, when she's old enough?*

My heart broke at that moment, and I sent up a quick prayer that God would always keep all our kids close by. Yet, even then, I knew that wasn't realistic. My heart also ached knowing that someday my sweet daughter would struggle with feelings of rejection, since she was rejected by her biological mother. I swore then I'd always remind Judah of my love, Brooke's love, and God's love—and I prayed that would be enough.

On the fifteen-hour flight home, there was a whole lot of fussing—both on the outside from Judah and inwardly from two weary parents. We were dealing with a baby girl who did not know us and did not want to be with us. She wouldn't come to me, even when Brooke needed a break. Thankfully, there were some Korean grannies who would hold Judah when Brooke needed to use the bathroom or wanted to eat. They'd walk up and down the aisle with Judah, and she was content.

Everyone at home was excited to meet our daughter, and she adjusted well, even with all the noise and busyness of her brothers. Everyone felt like they'd helped to bring her home, and they had.

From the start, I'd worried, *What if Judah never really bonds with me?* And after we brought her home, she didn't take to me for a little while. Then came the day when I was lying on the floor, playing with the other kids, and she just climbed onto my back. That was the best feeling, and she's been a daddy's girl ever since. Still, the process of adoption was, for me, a huge, huge leap of faith in a lot of different ways.

We'd been home with Judah eight months when we received a phone call from South Korea. They had another baby girl—Judah's sibling—and the agency wanted to give us the first option to adopt her.

I said yes immediately, which both shocked and delighted Brooke. How could I not say yes? But we had no idea how we'd get the money. We'd fundraised ourselves to death for Judah's adoption. After everyone had given so generously, we couldn't ask them for more. It took a huge step of faith to trust that God had a plan.

BROOKE

I'd been praying for a little girl for so long, and having Judah was just a beautiful gift. I remember walking into church after we brought Judah home and silently praying, *Thank you, God, for hearing my cry for a little girl.* And in the sweetest, gentlest way, I felt God speak to my heart: *Brooke, I didn't hear your cry. I heard her cry.* I really broke down then. He'd answered my prayer, yes. But God also reminded me of the cries of so many orphans who wanted and needed homes. I thought of Psalm 68:6: "God places the lonely in families; he sets the prisoners free and gives them joy" (NLT).

The stress of raising money and the joy of bringing Judah home was still fresh in our minds when the call from Korea came. I don't know why, but after talking to Todd about it, I called my daddy first. My dad is the most practical guy ever, but he told me, "If this is God, he'll pay for it." I clung to those words. "Well, God has to because y'all have wrung everyone else dry, you know," he added.

My mind was spinning, and my heart nearly burst as I met with the ladies at church that night. Since Todd and I were still trying to process the news, I hadn't told anybody else other than my dad. As I was preparing to leave our church meeting, one woman stopped me. She took my hand and pressed something into it, and said, "I don't know why, Brooke, but the Lord just told me that I need to give you this thousand dollars."

My mouth dropped open and tears filled my eyes. I pulled her into a hug. Clinging to that check, I told her, "Thank you, thank you."

That was the exact amount we needed to start the home study process again. I knew then that God had this. And that was just a tiny glimpse of the miracles to come.

Through the adoption agency, parents could post on an online board. During the process of adopting Judah, one lady connected with me. She and her husband had also adopted, and they had been praying for us. When this woman found out about our desire to adopt Judah's sister, she told her husband about it, especially how Todd had taken a great leap of faith in saying yes when he had no idea where the money would come from.

At the time, her husband was praying about selling his business to do something else. When this man we didn't know heard about our leap of faith, it touched his heart. He was especially humbled thinking of the poor Mississippi pastor with four kids living on a small salary who was willing to say yes. He told Todd later about how God used that to give him faith. He thought,

If this pastor can just step out in crazy faith, I can step out to what God is calling me to do. This man sold his business, and when he got the money for it, he turned around and paid for our entire adoption of Olive.

God did provide, and he again used his people to do it.

TODD

I remember getting the phone call from the agency and expecting to have to tell them that we had no money for the next step in the process of adopting Olive. Instead, they told me that the whole thing was paid for. Every penny. God showed his faithfulness again.

When we came home with Judah, she hollered and screamed; things were different with Olive. She didn't make the same fuss, but she looked so very sad. It just broke my heart seeing the sadness in her eyes.

When we brought Olive home, we were living in this little, tiny house. Olive's bed was in a small corner of our bedroom, and like her sister, she didn't connect with me at first, not even after being home for three weeks. That's when I asked everyone to leave the house except me and Olive. She screamed and cried. She was not real happy. Her eyes scanned the room, looking for Brooke. Finally, she came to me. That was a beautiful moment I'll never forget. And I would say that out of all the kids, Olive is most like me. We see life similarly and have a special bond.

The joy I have with my adopted daughters is the same joy all my kids bring to me. I know I'm not the perfect dad, but I do my best. Raising kids is really just a game of touch and go anyway. We all do the best we can to try and love our kids. I tell them I'm sorry. When our kids get in trouble and I overreact, I apologize for that.

Brooke and I are doing our best to let our daughters know how much they are loved. We're also open with them. We don't try to hide anything about their adoption. We've explained to them that they didn't cost us any money. We did not buy them. We did pay money, but it was to make sure they had food and medical care, and also for all the paperwork and funds so the agency can continue to help other children.

Judah is playful and sassy, and Olive is more serious. Sometimes when I'm sitting on the couch, Olive just climbs up next to me and wants to play with my hair and talk. They are fully my girls. I love the connection.

Olive also comes to me when she's upset or anxious, and she counts on my reassurance when her spirit is hurt or something happens. There's no difference between them and our other kids. They are mine. Completely mine. And they have my heart.

BROOKE

We're all adopted into the family of God. It's such a beautiful story, and we get to share it. We are forever thankful that God opened our hearts to adoption. I am honored to be the mother of these two girls. Adoption is from the heart of God.

My girls clearly look different from us, and we tell our girls their story over and over, showing that it's a beautiful thing. Yet, at the same time, adoption is born out of loss, and children have to process that.

Because of our girls, we also see race and equality in America differently. I understand when people say they don't see color—they're trying to say that they see everyone the same. But as parents of two Korean daughters, I've discovered it's good to see and appreciate color and differences. Not everyone has to fit inside the same box. We *should* see color. Seeing it helps us to better understand what is happening to others and to stand up for them.

God spoke to my heart about this. He made everybody vastly different for a reason. If we choose not to see these differences, we are choosing not to care about God's creations. And that breaks my heart.

On occasion someone will point out something different about our girls—mostly other kids. I like to point out things that are different about me, and we try to help them see that all of us are different. We try to build up our girls and their unique strengths.

We pray for their birth mom. We pray for their foster moms. From the time they were little, we've talked about how they've had three moms. One who loved them enough to give them life. Another who loved them until they got here. And me. I'm their forever mom, even though I'm far from perfect.

We're hoping that someday we can take them back to Korea, and that they'll at least get the chance to meet their foster moms and to know their culture. How amazing would that be?

Adoption is so worth it, but it's not easy. And it wasn't easy for God. He paid the ultimate price so we could be adopted into his family. I would have never thought when I was an eighteen-year-old girl getting married that this would be my story. But God writes the best stories if we listen. He really does.

TODD

People have asked me after concerts, "Why did you choose to adopt?" First of all, just them asking that question is a win. The idea that we can let others know about the beauty of adoption is special to us.

The best way I know how to answer them is that this is just how our family was supposed to come together. We didn't have fertility issues. And yes, we are people of faith and believe in adoption, but we don't feel like it's a mandate from God and that everyone has to do it. It just felt right for us. It's a win to know that, because of our story, others could open their homes to adopt or give to support those in the process of adopting.

It's also a win for our girls to know how much they are loved. Brooke and I are so thankful for everyone who made it possible for the girls to join our family, especially the girls' foster mothers. When they enter this process, those mamas know the end result, but they still love those babies anyway.

Olive's mom was especially broken to release Olive to us, and she followed us all the way down to the car. Seeing her outside of the car window crying, it struck me that this is how love really does work. Love is this insane cycle of one person breaking to make somebody else whole. Eventually your time comes to give away a really valuable, meaningful piece of yourself.

If you surrender yourself to love, there are always going to be times when you're the one being made whole and also times when you're the one breaking. And that's the win. Breaking and being made whole in the name of love is always a win.

WINS FOR TODAY

✓ We win when we understand God's heart for adoption.

✓ We win when we step out in faith to follow God's call to support orphans, whether by opening our homes or helping adoptive families.

✓ We win when we pray for those impacted by adoption. Birth parents, foster parents, adoptive parents, adoption workers, kids and their siblings— they all need our prayers.

✓ We win when we understand that sometimes we have to break to make another person whole—that's true love, true sacrifice.

✓ We win when we understand God's sacrifice to make us a part of *his* family. Adoption takes sacrifice for families to be joined together—both physical families and spiritual ones.

CHAPTER 5

Lord, Why Don't You Answer My Prayer?

BROOKE

After adopting the girls, I talked Todd into having one more baby. When you have five kids what's one more, right? Hosea was my biggest baby at birth, but right away I knew something was wrong. That baby couldn't nurse, couldn't eat. And, as months went by, he didn't gain weight. I went to doctor after doctor. I went to a breastfeeding specialist, driving two hours to see her. We still didn't know why he couldn't eat. It was almost like I was strangling him. I tried breastfeeding him for six weeks, but when he didn't gain any weight, I knew we had to try something else.

I was a mess. I tried every bottle, every formula, every nipple. It reached the point where Todd wouldn't let me feed Hosea because I would break down crying. I'd see my baby gasping, trying to swallow, and anxiety would fill me. I'd have to leave the room. As Todd tried to feed him, I'd just walk the halls and pray.

I was bawling one day, not knowing what to do. As a mother, you're supposed to be able to feed your baby. One day, our third son, Shepard, who was around eight at the time, came to comfort me. He said, "Mama, maybe that's why God made him so big when he was born—because he's not able to grow now."

I'd cry out to God, "Why are you letting my baby suffer

when I'm praying?" My heart ached. My stomach was all knotted up. Anger coursed through me. I was angrier with God than I'd ever been.

I'll be honest. When people said, "Oh, you can't get angry at God," I'd get mad at them too. I'd tell them, "David, from the Bible, got angry at God. How could I not be angry? Why would God let my baby suffer while I am praying? While I'm believing in a miracle?"

Hosea had a feeding tube put in, and they put him on a daily home health check and weighed him every day. I went to the doctor literally every two days, bawling, with my baby. We took him to the neurologist, and they couldn't find anything wrong. They sent us to an ear, nose, and throat doctor. They sent us to get Hosea an MRI. Finally, they sent us to Jackson, Mississippi, for a swallow study to see if Hosea was aspirating his food. The doctor had put off doing that, because he believed if Hosea was aspirating he'd have pneumonia. Still, his nurse urged him to do it, and not knowing what else to do, he agreed and sent a referral.

When we finally had the swallow study done, the doctor was so shocked with the results he would not let us leave with our baby. Hosea was aspirating so badly that every time he'd try to swallow milk, it would be pulled down into his lungs. The hospital kept his study because they'd never seen anything like it before. And that's why Hosea would never latch. He was literally gagging himself every time he swallowed.

The doctor looked at the results of the swallow study, turned to me, and said, "This is a miracle. How could this baby not be sick when he's aspirating so badly? He should be so sick with aspiration pneumonia."

I really broke down then. I'd been so angry with God, but the whole time, he was protecting my baby. I didn't know it then, but God was working and stretching my faith too. I was about to go into one of the worst mental battles of my life, and this was part of faith building. God was trying to teach me and grow me. But at that moment, when I heard the doctor's words, I knew God was there. He'd been there all along.

TODD

I've never felt more helpless than when I had to take my child from my weeping wife, and then try to feed a baby who was choking as he ate.

Ever since we were married, I'd tried to make sure Brooke was okay. And then, when we had our kids, I'd make sure they were okay too. And even as things got more serious, and Hosea was starving, I tried to act like everything was going to be fine for the sake of Brooke. But I was afraid. Honestly, I was legitimately scared that Hosea was going to die. I've never told anyone that. But in my mind, that fear had me by the throat. I'd hold Brooke and tell her everything was going to be fine, and deep down I prayed it really would. I also had this hope that the next time I'd feed Hosea he would do better.

Once we figured out what was going on with Hosea, we learned we had to thicken up his food to the consistency of oatmeal. That was the only way his food would be heavy enough to go down into his stomach and not into his lungs. And only Brooke or I could feed him, because it had to be done a certain way.

It was almost like a science experiment. We had to mix everything up with this thickener, but that would make him constipated. So we had to add in this other stuff to help prevent that. And then we had to cut the nipples on the bottle so it could all go through. Thankfully, he started gaining weight.

I cried when we put all these components away once Hosea started eating solid food. It had been such a journey. We'd had a whole setup in the kitchen to make his food. Putting them away was proof of the miracle.

Hosea is eight years old now, and Brooke and I still have conversations about how much he eats. Hosea is literally the kid that never stops asking if it's okay to have a snack. And every time, we tell him *yes*.

It brings us joy to see him eat. It reminds us of God's faithfulness. Hosea's the one who goes back for seconds and thirds, and our hearts stretch when we see that—when we see what God has done.

BROOKE

After Hosea started eating, we had an appointment with the GI doctor because he wasn't getting any fluids. They wanted to put in a GI tube (gastrostomy tube inserted through the belly that brings nutrition directly to the stomach), but I didn't have peace about that. I talked to the speech therapist who was working with Hosea—training him to take things by mouth—and I talked to Todd. We knew if Hosea didn't keep eating by mouth now, it would be hard later, so we decided to wait.

The speech therapist told me, "Let's just keep doing what we're doing. If you don't feel at peace about it, and you've prayed about it, then you shouldn't have that GI tube put in."

We never went in to get the procedure done. Then slowly, over time, we started moving from the thick formula to feeding him applesauce. We noticed Hosea would swallow two or three times to get it down. He was self-adjusting. And soon he was able to eat everything, drink everything, just like my other kids.

Yet, if dealing with Hosea's health challenges wasn't hard enough, in the middle of all of this, I got pregnant with Louie. Hosea was only six months old, and it was a complete surprise.

With the stress of Hosea, my postpartum emotions, and getting pregnant again, I entered a downward spiral of fear and worry about things going wrong. After our struggles with Hosea, I grew increasingly afraid of bad things happening. I was thankful that my baby was doing so well, but I had no idea of the dark season that lay ahead.

———◆———

We knew Hosea's healing was a miracle. God sustained him, and then God healed him. It's a win when we know that the God who performed miracles in the Bible can still perform them now. There's no other explanation. It's also a win that Hosea eats the house down.

It's a win that even when we don't understand God, he doesn't abandon us. Ultimately, God knew the whole time I was angry and frustrated that our son was going to be fine. I had to learn to trust him. I had to learn to walk in faith.

WINS FOR TODAY

✓ We win when we place our kids in God's hands. We will never fully be able to protect our kids or make sure they're healthy.

✓ We win when we turn to one another for support. Even when we don't have all the answers, we can help and encourage one another. We can hold one another up.

✓ We win when we dare to have real emotions with God. He understands when we're disappointed or angry. He doesn't love us any less.

✓ We win when we believe in God's healing powers. He doesn't always choose to heal, but we can trust that he is able.

✓ We win when we walk in faith, even when we don't have immediate answers.

CHAPTER 6

The Valley of the Shadow of Death

BROOKE

Some of my earliest memories are going with my mother to nursing homes to pray. She moved from person to person, looking into each one's eyes, and really caring about their needs.

"Let's pray," Mama would say, and I would bow my head as I sat next to her. Mama modeled for me that no matter our needs, we could always take them to God in prayer.

I watched Mama pray and I took it to heart. Even when I was young, Jesus was the most important person to me. I loved Strawberry Shortcake, Care Bears, and Rainbow Brite, but Jesus was even more important to me than those.

I hugged my stuffed monkey, Chico, to my chest and told her, "Mama, I want to see Jesus. I want to see Jesus a lot."

My mama's eyes grew round and she grasped my arms. "You're scaring me, sweetie."

Later I overheard her talking to Daddy. "Oh my gosh. Something's going to happen to her. She says she wants to see Jesus."

"Nah, just calm down," Daddy said. "You know how dramatic she is."

I might have been dramatic, but I wasn't fooling one night when I told my mama that I didn't feel good. She touched her hand to my forehead. Her hand felt cool. Her eyes narrowed with concern, and then her hand moved to my cheeks. "Why, Brooke, you're burning up."

She helped me get into bed and tried to make me comfortable, but it was no use. Sickness weakened my body and fever burned like fire on my skin. I tossed and turned, and my arms and legs felt like they were filled with rocks. Heavy, too heavy. Mama leaned over me and placed a cool rag on my forehead. She tried to get me to sip water, but even that took too much energy.

I heard water filling the bathtub, and Mama lifted me and carried me there. She stripped me down and lowered me into the water. A thousand needles poked into my skin. I cried out and clung to her.

"No!" Ice bobbed in the water. I kicked my feet and tried to get out.

"I'm sorry, sweetie, we have to get the fever down. Please, Brooke—"

Pretty soon it got too hard to fight. I lay there as tears slipped down my mother's face. I heard her pray. Her words were desperate. "It's not going down. The fever's not going down," she mumbled to herself as she drew me up from the bathtub and wrapped a towel around me.

"Dear Jesus, touch this baby," she prayed as she carried me back to bed. "Please, heal her. Lord, I don't know what to do."

Her prayers continued, but the fever clung to me. I drifted off and then woke again, crying. Everything hurt. Sometime in the night I awoke and saw someone standing in front of me. It was a man, but not my daddy. I wasn't scared. I felt love, peace.

"Jesus," I whispered.

I'm going to take that fire from the Enemy and put it back on the Devil where it belongs. Jesus's words were calm, but he spoke with authority. I listened, and I knew everything was going to be all right. I drifted off to sleep again.

I'm not sure how much time passed, but I awoke and reached my hand toward my mama. "Mama, Jesus told me that he's going to take the fire that the Enemy put on me. He's going to put it back on the Devil where it belongs."

Mama leaned close, wiping the tears from her eyes. "What did you say, sweetie?"

"Listen, Mama. Jesus told me that he's going to take the fire that the Enemy put on me. He's going to put it back on the Devil where it belongs."

Even as I said the words, I could feel a change. The heat began to disappear. The ache started going too. Immediately, the fever left, and I knew Jesus had healed me. He had told me that it was going to be okay, and it was.

That day was just the beginning. God has continued to talk to my heart in gentle ways. It's not an audible voice, but I can hear him. The trouble comes when there are other things that overshadow Jesus's voice. In my life, that has been anxiety and fear.

There's a vine that grows in the South called kudzu. You see it all over Meridian and other parts of Mississippi. You see it covering sides of hills, climbing up trees and power poles, covering old houses until they look like a mound of green. It's said that once a kudzu vine takes root and starts growing, it can grow a foot a day. And each tendril can start its own plant. It's invasive, to say the least.

When I was young, the Enemy put the fire of fever upon me,

but as I grew older, the Enemy planted kudzu in my heart with the roots of fear and anxiety.

My mind tends to focus on the bad things. First of all, like Todd, it probably didn't help that there seemed to be so many rules at church. I've believed in Jesus since I was very young, but I probably "got saved" four hundred times growing up. If I went out and did anything wrong—or something I thought was wrong—I thought I needed to pray and dedicate my life to Jesus again. I wanted to make sure that I was good with him and there wasn't something I'd done that would keep me from getting into heaven. I was afraid that if I told a lie and then got hit by a car, I'd burn in hell.

As the years passed, my anxiety and fear transferred to my kids. I worried over every little thing, and I didn't want anything bad to happen to them. When Hosea was six months old and I became pregnant with Louie, the fear and anxiety really took root. Even though Todd and I had a house brimming with life, all I could think about was death.

The worries about Hosea were real worries, but even when he started doing better, I was certain I was going to be the one to die. Lies continually filled my mind: *You're not gonna rock your grandbabies. You're not gonna see your kids grow up.* Not seeing them grow up has always been my biggest fear.

During my pregnancy with Louie, I experienced pain in my breast, and immediately I was sure I had cancer. This belief so consumed me that I bruised myself feeling for lumps. Black and blue marks covered my chest. Then, with this new pregnancy, I started bleeding, and a good bit. That brought all types of fears.

When I went in for my first pregnancy appointment, the

nurse couldn't find the baby's heartbeat with the Doppler ultrasound. The lies spoke to me again: *I told you, you're going to lose this baby.*

But the Spirit of God inside me spoke differently. Pushing through the worried thoughts, God's voice was strong: *Declare life. Speak life.*

The nurse seemed to panic a little, and she hurried to get the doctor. While waiting, I mentally skimmed through every scripture I could think of, speaking them aloud.

The doctor came in, sadness filling her face. "Brooke, I'm sorry. It looks as if we don't have good news here. But let me check."

She's trying to prepare me for losing the baby.

The doctor tried with the Doppler, but there was only silence. My hands gripped the sides of the exam table. Tears filled the corners of my eyes, and I squeezed them tight.

Then, seemingly coming out of nowhere, the heartbeat sounded. *Thump, thump, thump.* I released the breath I'd been holding, and smiles filled the faces of the doctor and the nurse. "Well, there it is," the doctor said.

But even though things started to go better with my pregnancy, the fears didn't end. I struggled with anxiety every day of that pregnancy. The depression was so debilitating that I couldn't care for my kids. Todd had to get extra help to come in.

One of my fears was that I had ALS (Lou Gehrig's disease). It seems silly now, but the fear started when I saw my tongue moving in a strange way. I was sitting in the car with the kids as Todd ran into the store. I was playing around with them, and when I looked in the mirror it looked as if my tongue was wiggling like little worms.

I turned to my kids and asked them to stick out their tongues. I wanted to see if their tongues did the same thing. None of their tongues did. Only mine. It kept wiggling in this strange way. My kids still tease me to this day, remembering how I told them over and over, "Stick out your tongues. Stick out your tongues."

When I looked up that symptom, there was only one thing that it pointed to: ALS, a neurodegenerative, neuromuscular disease that results in the loss of motor neurons that control voluntary muscles.

I'll never forget the feeling of dread that came over me when I saw this search result. I can't describe it. It was as if every ounce of joy or any hope I had was gone. Darkness and depression came over me.

Once I read the symptoms, I was consumed with the thought. I read everything I could about ALS. I watched documentaries about people who had ALS, and I said over and over in my mind: *That's me. That's me.*

The thing about ALS is that there is no test for it. There is no test you can run that says you don't have it. So, even though I had this great fear, God put me in a position of having to trust him. It was as if he was reminding me: *You're not going to be able to run to the doctor to take away your fear, Brooke.*

I went from doctor to doctor, and even though they couldn't find anything wrong, I was convinced of my illness. I went to a neurologist who tried to assure me. "If you did have ALS, Brooke, you would have seen more symptoms by now," he said. "By now, you wouldn't be able to talk well." He almost smiled when he said that because I'm a talker. I talk a lot. "I don't think you have it."

I felt a little bit better that moment, but his last words stuck with me: "We'll just have to wait and see if there are any changes. We'll just have to watch."

I knew there was more I could do than that. I knew I could pray too. So I prayed. A lot.

I knew with ALS that your speech starts to go because it's muscular, so then I became concerned with every word that came from my mouth. Every time I fumbled with my words, I'd hear that voice in my head: *See, you have this. You know you have it. You know what's going to happen to you.*

Whenever I'd see friends at church who were happy, I'd start crying because I thought I'd never be happy again. Then, even though I'm a talker, I was afraid to talk to people for fear that I'd mess up my words. I started to isolate myself, locking myself in my room. I would get a book and read it out loud—the entire book—just to prove to myself that I could get through it without screwing up the words. I'd also go outside and look to the sky and pray. I'd pace and pray, but really it was an obsession.

I tried to walk around and clean the house and do normal things, but then seeing photos of my kids would cause me to break down. And then my leg started dragging. I had a baby on my hip, and I was pregnant, but even Todd noticed the way I was walking. He told the doctor I looked like one of those zombies from *The Walking Dead*.

I went to another neurologist, and in the waiting room I saw someone who had ALS. Seeing how far the disease had progressed, I began to comprehend that I should be like that . . . but I wasn't. Still, I couldn't shake the anxiety and fear.

I did my best through this downward spiral, clinging to God, but that was literally all I could do. I had to listen to worship music to go to sleep. And I needed to be with Todd at all times. I found my security in him. He was the only one who really understood all that was going on. Most of the kids were in school, so I even went to work with him.

I had to untangle myself from those fears. I remember being pregnant and rocking Hosea, who was doing a little better, while begging God, "Please, give me more time, please." The tears wouldn't stop coming. "Please, please, God."

I needed to change, but I didn't have the power to make it happen. I remember praying over and over, "God, I am so tired of being afraid. I am so tired of it. I want to be free. I want to be free. I'm so tired of it."

When I couldn't gain control of my fear and anxiety, I thought about checking myself into inpatient treatment. Todd was uncomfortable with the idea, but we didn't know what else to do. Both Todd and my mama had a hard talk with me. "We think you need help," Mama said as she squeezed my hands.

I thought about my kids. Eagan, Asher, and Shep were old enough to know what was going on. Shep was nine, Asher ten, and Eagan thirteen. Hosea was still a baby, and Judah and Olive were six and five. I couldn't care for them, and for them to see me in such a mess wasn't helping anything. I began to believe that maybe I did need to be hospitalized. It meant leaving all my children in the care of others, but I wasn't doing well caring for them anyway.

Then, right before I was going to check into the hospital, my mama suggested I go see her nurse practitioner. Instead of simply listening to my list of problems and fears, the nurse practitioner looked at me with compassion. "You're a young mother with a lot of kids at home," she said, "and you're dealing with postpartum hormones and now pregnancy hormones. You're not crazy. You're exhausted. And your body is spent."

She was a Christian, and she spoke to me from a Christian perspective. She gave me a lot of hope. She didn't make me feel like I was losing my mind. She told me she understood why I was worried, and she got me in with a new neurologist the next day for a checkup just for my peace of mind.

Her words helped me. *Could it be I'm not dying? Could it be that hormones have a lot to do with this? And maybe I'm just really exhausted too.*

The nurse practitioner prescribed medication for anxiety and depression that was safe during pregnancy, and within a few weeks, I noticed a change. During my darkest days, I was sure I would never be happy or peaceful again. But a year later, I felt like myself—something I never thought would happen. Louie was born on the first day of spring, and it was so spiritually significant. I felt like I'd entered a new season. Louie was such a surprise and such a good baby.

As I started to hope again, I began to understand not to let those negative thoughts take root. Because of what I went through, I'm also compassionate for others. I understand them better, understand their struggles.

Even as I was coming out of the darkness, I cried out to God: "Why would you do this to me? I was begging you to help me."

And I felt God speak to my heart. I felt him say, *Brooke, you asked me for freedom, but what you really wanted was relief. Freedom is a different thing. Real freedom is costly, and it's not easy. But you've learned now how to overcome.*

In the process, I've learned to battle those thoughts. I've

learned to stop them before they take root. Whenever a bad thought starts in my mind, I begin thinking about Scripture instead. I pray and ask God for help in controlling my thoughts. I don't give them room to grow. I also tell Todd or a friend and ask them to pray for me.

There were times when every ten seconds those bad thoughts would be there, but the more I stopped them the less often they came—like every ten minutes. Then only a few times a day. And then the day came when I realized I had gone a whole day without worrying I was going to die or that something serious was wrong with me. The kudzu can't grow and spread if you rip up the vine right from the start. The same is true for negative thoughts.

It's not like everything changed overnight. There was not one miraculous moment. The medications helped to stabilize my hormones, yes. But also, day by day, I learned that I had to renew my mind as the Bible says in the book of Romans.[1] I had to push out the lies of the Enemy.

The Devil wants to hurt us, and if he can't take our lives, he will try to take our peace. The Devil's lies were the ones I had been listening to, lies that told me I was sick and was going to die. These lies had robbed me of peace and happiness with my family.

I had to choose faith over fear. And then, with that faith I had to start looking for the joy. Joy is found in my kids, in my husband, and in the love of friends. Joy is found in God and his good plans for me. Looking for the joy takes my focus off all the things that make me anxious. But it wasn't easy then, and it still takes work now.

TODD

I know it was devastating for Brooke having to deal with her anxiety and depression, but it was also really devastating for me. Mostly because it started out so small, just this little thing with her tongue. We got to the place where it was so bad, she could not function day to day. Fear and anxiety had a grip on her.

She'd cry and say that God didn't love her. Then she'd go outside and pray, and pray so obsessively that I'd have to go get her. "That's enough, Brooke. That's enough praying."

We'd go to all these doctors, and they'd tell us she was fine. I honestly didn't know how to handle it—her and all the kids. I didn't want to leave her, leave our marriage, but I also began to feel like I couldn't do it. I didn't know if I had it in me, because every day was a miserable battle.

Sometimes I'd lash out at her. "You're not sick. You're fine. You know, everything's fine. Look at you. Even if you did have ALS, it would have progressed at least a little by now. It's literally like you get caught up in that, and nothing that you see and know to be true registers as the truth."

She'd come to the church office with me because she couldn't stay home alone or be with the kids when they were home. And it did get to the point where her mama and I considered putting her in a facility. I tried to hold on to hope that it wouldn't go that far. I'm the type of person who finds the positive in any situation and hangs on to that. But it was really bad.

And the thing is, I don't remember when she came out of it. I do remember her getting on some antidepressants that helped.

And then, little by little, all those fears and anxieties that she clung to seemed to fade. There are times she still struggles with anxiety and depression, but she's learning to not let it take hold. And that's important.

All of us want to have a life of joy and a life absent of trouble, but that's not going to happen on this earth. A lot of times when God sets us free from our struggles, that doesn't mean he's freed us from the temptation of those things or from the draw of those things.

Since then, the win has been not only that she's better but also that we stuck it out—as hard as it was, we stuck it out. Honestly, every major issue we've ever gone through in our relationship has made us better. Going through those things, we gain more connectedness and intimacy at a heart level. We've formed a stronger bond as we've come through. It's like two plastic pieces melted together and then solidified again. The breaking and fire that could have destroyed us have actually made us more unified, more one.

I can talk to people about many things, but Brooke can meet someone who's really struggling and speak to their heart better than I ever could.

She can tell them, "It might not be tomorrow. It might not be the next day. You may end up getting on medication, and that's okay. I know, because I've been there, and I'm still there." She opens her heart to hurting people, and they accept it because they can hear the truth in her words.

This part of our life is as important as all the other parts. This victory for Brooke is as important as my win on *The Voice*. More important. In fact, another song that I just helped to write—and one that I'll be recording—is called "Victories." It's about everyday people celebrating victories that only heaven sees. There are no gold medals or confetti, but there is a reason to celebrate. Victories like these are worth celebrating.

In the song, there's a verse about a guy who was in a car accident, and the doctors tell him, "You might not ever walk a step," but then he takes the first step. That's a victory. In another verse, a man is sitting on the couch with his wife, and he asks her, "Is there any way you can forgive me?" And they work through it. That's a victory.

Those small victories are so much of our lives. Remember to celebrate them, to see the joy in them. Sometimes a victory happens overnight with a vote on national television. And sometimes it happens so gradually you don't realize how far things have come until one day the battle is won.

BROOKE

I used to feel ashamed for thinking I was going to die. Things started to change when I was finally able to open up to Todd and tell him about my struggles. I confessed some of the dark things that were coming to my mind.

At first, because of the way I grew up, I believed it was shameful to share my weaknesses. I was afraid people would think that I didn't pray enough, and they would judge me for that. In the Christian community, there is sometimes a stigma if you have mental struggles, as if you don't have enough faith. But once I was able to open up to Todd about this, I knew I could open up to him about anything and everything. I still go to him. Todd can bring a calm to me when I need it most.

Just as I've learned to trust Todd with my anxious thoughts, I've noticed that when I tell my story, the shame I feel is gone; others, too, feel less ashamed. When you can't share it, the Enemy shames, telling you that you're the only one and something is wrong with you. But when you tell people, it's freeing. It's been so freeing for me to share my struggles and lead others to find help.

Again, I can see why God brought Todd and me together. Todd is my safe place, even with my emotions. He's such a gift to me. He's one of the only people who can comfort me when I'm losing it.

In this season, after Todd won *The Voice*, there's been a lot of change. Things have been crazy. A lot is going on. Lately I have been battling a little harder with this. And the old Brooke would have had a pity party. I would have asked, "God, why do I have to struggle and battle anxiety and fear? Why is this so hard?" But during a recent prayer, I felt a shift in my perspective. I began to see this battle as an opportunity for *victory*, an opportunity for God to grow me and teach me.

You see, God knows more about what I'm capable of than I do. He knows what I need to go through so I can become an overcomer. He knows who I need to reach. And what tools I will need for the next level.

I have to trust that when I walk through any battle, it's for a greater purpose. And the other side is going to be so *great* that God chose to allow me to walk through it. God is good. Our stories are good. And if they ain't good yet, then we still can't give up, because our stories ain't over. And that is a win.

Maybe you struggle with fearful thoughts. I'm here to tell you there can be victory. You don't have to live in fear. You don't have to let those fears control you. Find someone you can turn to for help. Root out those negative thoughts before they go deep. There can be joy on the other side of your fears. I know, because I've experienced it.

WINS FOR TODAY

- ✓ We win when we listen for God's voice, for life and peace, instead of listening to fearful thoughts.
- ✓ We win when we can share our struggles with others, when we can help them see that they are not alone.
- ✓ We win when we learn to overcome and not just settle for an easy fix.
- ✓ We win when we learn to battle our negative thoughts, when we cut them out before they take root.
- ✓ We win when we choose to think about all the good things God has given us; doing so brings faith and joy.
- ✓ We win when we see our battles as opportunities for victory, opportunities for God to grow us and teach us.

CHAPTER 7

Discovering Ourselves

TODD

When I was eleven my family moved to Kosciusko, Mississippi, which is almost right in the middle of the state. The town is known as the birthplace of civil rights leader James Meredith and television personality Oprah, but all I knew back then was that life was about singing in church and playing in the dirt.

In Kosciusko, we lived in a rural setting—not that Grenada is urban, but back there we at least lived in town. Living outside of town, I developed a love for walking in the woods and hiking. The Natchez Trace is a popular motorway trail that goes through the area. It's a beautiful place. Also, we didn't have other families around—there was just my parents, my brother and sister, and me. Looking back, that time in Kosciusko was when my love for nature took root in my heart. It was when my love for music took root too.

Like I mentioned, at that county fair when I was nine and living in Grenada, I sang "He Grew the Tree" and won second place. But later, I sang at church-run talent shows. My dad would always lead the music for the most part, and I would sing. We were in Kosciusko for only three years, but there are a few things that stand out, like the fact that I sang the song "I Just Started Living" a thousand times.

The funny part about singing that song as a boy was that I had no life experience to go with the lyrics. The song talked about having a brand-new life and changing direction from the strife of the past. What did I know at that age?

That song came from my environment. It's a southern gospel song, and I was from the South in a little country church. There was this young woman who came to church, and she'd play piano for me. I sang that same song nearly every Sunday. Then one day I got up to sing that song, and I couldn't because the key was bad. Of course, it wasn't actually the key; my voice had changed. So, instead of moving to a different song, we switched the key around because people just loved the song. I supposed they loved my voice, too, but I didn't think about that then. I sang a lot of Ray Boltz. I sang "Watch the Lamb" every Easter—that was a popular song back then too—and "I Will Praise the Lord."

In Kosciusko, I started singing at our denomination's state-wide talent competition: Teen Talent. And if I won, I advanced to nationals at the biannual General Assembly conventions. I would always sing or share a poem or draw something—but I got the most attention for my singing.

Kosciusko was also where my dad became my pastor. Good or bad, I felt a bit of the pressure of being part of the pastor's family. And it was the first time I lived without Granny. She had passed away shortly before we moved. Near the end of our time in Kosciusko, I mourned her not being around. I was really broken, and I'd just cry.

At age fourteen we moved to Meridian, and I was always part of the church worship team. You already know how God moved in my life from there.

Connecting to the message and the meaning of worship music has helped me to connect with music in general. Even if I haven't lived the same experiences in the songs I'm listening to or singing, I can feel the pain, the joy, the heartbeat of the words. I can listen to a song that reflects a loss or heartache, and I soon feel tears on my cheeks. Music touches my soul in a special way.

In my teenage years, I started listening to country music. I connected with country music, but I also enjoyed other genres. My brother and I got into trouble because my dad found out that we had been listening to Bon Jovi, Poison, and Cinderella. I remember Daddy sitting us down and pointing out lyrics that went against God's Word. He talked about not filling our minds with things that would take away our peace. Yeah, we had to destroy those CDs. Fortunately, country music was tamer and approved by my parents.

I loved Alan Jackson, Garth Brooks, and George Strait through the nineties. I've always loved Phil Collins, U2, and, even though I didn't fall as far as my friends into an obsession, Nirvana. I've also always loved bluegrass music, which no one understood. And folk songs. I remember one time when I was driving down the road with friends, they raked me over the coals because I was listening to John Denver. I love John Denver. Who doesn't love John Denver?

Unlike most guys my age, I also fell in love with the soul singers. I was moved when I'd listen to Bill Withers singing "Ain't No Sunshine." And even back then, when I heard Mahalia Jackson singing "There Is a Balm in Gilead," I heard her pain, and also her hope. I heard it with the deepest part of me.

Maybe that was part of living in Mississippi, too, since there was so much struggle with the civil rights movement—so much pain and longing to know true freedom by the African Americans in our community. Also, Mississippi isn't a rich place. So when people sang about hardship, I understood it from observing the world around me. If you can't get the opportunity, you don't get the job. If you don't get the job, you don't have the money. If you don't have the money, you don't have the food or the clothes. And then you end up singing: "There is a balm in Gilead to make the wounded whole; there is a balm in Gilead to save a sin-sick soul."

I've always challenged myself to do runs and add musical lines or responses, like the gospel soul singers I admire do—you know, things that white folks can't normally do. A run is when a singer starts off at a very high note and drops quickly through the scale down to a very low note or vice versa. A call-and-response is where a phrase in a line of music is answered by a different phrase. While these things are common in gospel music, they're hard to do, but I taught myself how. I'd practice by slowing down a run and singing every note by itself. Over time, I suppose I trained my voice.

Because I was practicing these things, they started coming out when I led worship too. It became my style over time. The more comfortable I became with music, the more I started ad-libbing and responding. I tell people who ask me for advice that if they want to sing, then they have to just go ahead and let it all out. You can't halfway do it. It's better to just give it your all than try to be too polished.

Music is so creative. People put these lyrics together, add a beat, and all of a sudden, you're crying. Even though many amazing singers and musicians may not know God, you can see the creative God in them to be able to do that. As the years passed, I realized that music helped me understand and connect with those beyond the church walls.

A couple of years ago, I felt God nudging me to look beyond the type of songs I've always sung and the type of crowd I've always sung to. I still loved God and his people with all my heart, but I felt as if he was asking me to pause and realize there was a great big world out there with people who needed hope.

I suppose it began when I started to connect with the emotion in songs and not be so concerned with whether or not they were Christian. I also understood that if I only sang Christian songs, there would be a whole lot of people who would tune me out immediately. If God gave me the ability to sing, I wanted to use that ability to connect with all people. I wanted them to want to know more about me and where my joy comes from.

Over time, I had a feeling something was going to change with my music—that change needed to happen—but I didn't know what.

BROOKE

I've always known that I'm a big personality, and what you see is what you get. When I met Todd, I thought he was an extreme extrovert. Looking back, I think he was self-conscious about his weight and always tried to be who people expected him to be to make them like him. He's still the same man I married, but he understands more about himself now. It's been a good journey to watch, and one that's inspired me.

While I never cared much about what people thought of what I did or said, I was always concerned with what they thought about how I looked. This was especially true when I started going gray in my late twenties. I didn't like the gray, and I covered it because I felt ashamed. I literally felt ashamed when people said offhandedly, "Oh, you have gray roots."

"Yeah. Okay. Yes, I do," I would say, feeling embarrassed. And so I kept paying money to get my hair done every two weeks.

I covered up the gray until about two years ago. I thought, *You know, if men can be sexy with gray hair, why can't women?* I was tired of women being told that we have to look a certain way. And that's when I decided to let my natural color come out. It was also freeing to cut my hair off in a pixie, to help the gray grow out easier. I hid behind my hair most of my life. Finally I decided I liked being the real me.

Letting my hair be its natural color was a small thing that has turned into a big win. I now know that I've got to own who I am—who God created me to be. Being yourself authentically is attractive. That draws people in. After Todd won *The Voice*, people also messaged me. They saw my joy. They told me they could tell I was a fun person. In fact, this whole book project started because our coauthor thought I looked like someone she'd want to get to know better, even as she was cheering Todd on with his singing.

Seeing Todd discover himself and grow into who God created him to be has also drawn people to him—his authentic self. And I know God has brought us together for a reason. I'm kind of like the gas, and Todd's the brakes. I have all these crazy ideas, and Todd sometimes gets pushed along for the ride. But during the journey, he falls in love with most of my ideas.

Todd keeps me from totally embarrassing the mess out of myself, like when I'm getting a little too far out there, while I urge him to think outside the box and just try.

TODD

When it comes to change, sometimes things have to build and build before you're ready for it. The same was true with my weight loss. It was something I always struggled with, until I knew enough was enough.

Sometimes people think there has to be a big tipping point before change comes. Honestly, for me, there was just one day when I thought to myself, *I'm too big. I gotta change.* I don't want to take away from the impact of this book, but there's no dramatic story behind my decision. Like I said, there just came a time when enough was enough.

I've always loved food and thought about food. I didn't think I could control my eating until I did. I didn't start losing weight in the healthiest way. I just counted calories, whether it was two hundred calories for a Twinkie or two hundred calories worth of vegetables. I thought the number was more important than what I chose to eat, which I know now isn't true.

I did better as I went and eventually lost over one hundred pounds. And along the way, I got healthy. At that time, I felt like there were a lot of things in my life that were a bit out of control, and so I thought maybe I could at least do something about my weight. Once I started counting calories, I started to see results. Then, with the results, I started to think more about my overall health. As I worked on self-control, my inner man grew stronger.

Not that I don't still struggle, but I'm learning to overcome. Through my journey, I've learned that life is not just about being healthy; it's about being whole. It's about looking at who God created each of us to be. For me, being whole is staying healthy, connecting with God in nature, serving and loving people, and singing. Singing songs that speak truth to a listener's heart gives me access to speak into their life too.

Sometimes it feels selfish to pursue the things you feel make you whole, whether that's going to the gym or leaving everything behind to go for a hike. But the more I understood myself, the more I realized what I needed.

When it came to hiking and heading out into nature, first, I loved it. And second, when I'm in the woods or running the trails, I find a special level of peace. I feel close to God when I'm out there. I see his creative power, and it gives me delight. I find fulfillment in the woods, just like I find fulfillment being with my wife and family. As time passes, I know that's who God created me to be.

Yet sometimes taking time to discover who you are seems selfish. For so long I didn't want to let people down. As a people pleaser, I worried they'd be disappointed in me. But knowing what my soul needs, I've learned to give myself permission to step away. It's a battle within my mind, really. Having been a pastor for so many years and having a large family, I know there's always something I could be doing or maybe should be doing. But I also know I'm better in all my roles when I take time to connect with God and find that inner peace.

Even though I've found happiness, I've discovered this journey wasn't just about me being happy. Yes, happiness and joy are part of this journey with the Lord, but the end result is truly experiencing wholeness in who God made me to be and not just trying to please other people. The steps for me were to lose weight, to spend more time outdoors, and to take this music venture. We each have to do what we believe will make us whole and not worry about what others might think.

Brooke and I go off to the woods for a week around our anniversary every year. Over the years, a few people have commented, "Well, those kids would probably sure love to go on that trip with you."

I tell them, "I'm sure they would, but they're not going. Brooke and I need this time."

When life is challenging, like it is for all of us, getting away is hard. There were times when I would worry about what was going on at church or what was going on with the family, and I'd have to make a conscious decision to take care of those things in a different way at a different time. We still love God even if we miss church once in a while, but some people find that hard to believe.

Looking back, I see that all these changes within me were preparation for what God wanted to do in my life. God knew I needed this peace—this freedom—for the change to come. It took having that freedom for me to step away and try out for *The Voice*. I'm continuing to walk in that peace and freedom now as I step away from full-time church service to pursue music.

I've made a huge change in my life to pursue music, and it's not a "me" thing at all. With my wife and kids, it's a "nine other people" thing. And that's not even scratching the surface of who else is involved. There are people in the music industry who are impacted. There are also friends and fans of my music.

As I'm pursuing wholeness, and using my gifts and talents, I'm able to reach the world with God's love in ways I never dreamed possible. People pleasing would have held me back, but as I've looked up to God and focused on pleasing him, everything has changed for the good.

Don't get me wrong, I'm scared to death as far as how things are going to turn out with my music. But I also feel a lot of freedom walking into what's next. If God can take me from being a pastor of a small church in Mississippi to winning *The Voice*, what else does he have up his sleeve? Anything is possible.

With me moving away from pastoral ministry toward music, there are those who may be thinking, *This guy's just gotten too big for his britches.* But I've been on this journey with God for a while. I've known for a long time that I was going to be moving away from traditional ministry; I just didn't know how. Yet God did show me how as I took steps of faith and followed him. I thought I was simply trying to get a nagging wife off my back when I tried out for *The Voice*, but God showed me that this was part of my story. It was part of my family's story. It was part of his story.

God's been on this journey all along. To a great degree, when I was at *The Voice* studio in California, God gave me a lot of opportunities to love people and be kind to them.

———•———

Everything we've learned from all those years of pastoring and growing comes down to this: first, the gospel—the truth of God's Word—is good news, even though many people use it to point out everyone else's sins; and second, people just want to be loved.

God has opened a lot of doors for me to build relationships with a lot of people beyond the church walls. My theology is Jesus and love. Love is a balance of grace and truth. And, no matter how people present themselves, if you strip everything away, there's just a person with a spirit and a heart. Because of that, my unloving actions or words can be detrimental. Jesus is all about making people whole, just as he's making me whole.

The gospel frees you, and it's good. I'm not saying it frees you to do whatever you want, but that it frees you—your spirit—to be who you're supposed to be. So this is what I offer to those I meet: here's Jesus, and here's the love of Jesus.

If you're talking to a Christian and the conversation sends you down a path of brokenness or makes you feel you're less of a person, that's not the gospel. Sometimes as Christians we damage people more than we help them. You can see evidence of that in the world right now.

Each of us needs to understand that the sacrifice of Jesus and the love of Jesus are what changes us. Left on our own, we're never going to be good enough to get into heaven—no one is. But over time, Jesus's love will change things, and you will have the strength to not give in to the desires to do the things that are detrimental.

We are changed by the power of God and the power of the gospel. I'm not a great theologian. So people certainly don't have to listen to a thing I have to say. But I can sum up the power of the gospel this way: the more time you spend with Jesus, the more Jesus will change you. You don't have to change a thing to come to him. You can just come right where you are now, today.

I've known Jesus from my earliest days, and because of my own insecurities, for a time I focused on what I thought would make the people of the church happy rather than what would bring God joy. So during *The Voice* competition, I intentionally chose music that shared both a story and an emotion rather than just thinking I had to do Christian songs. And because of this, there were those on set and behind the scenes who expressed that they enjoyed getting to know me and felt drawn to me. They felt God's love from me even before they realized I was a pastor. I like that. That's a win.

For me, the ultimate test of being a God-follower is, after someone spends time with you, that person feels that you honestly love them and love God. We're all going to disappoint people at some point, but can you be known as someone who demonstrates love? I think each of us can.

WINS FOR TODAY

✓ We win when we look at what interests us and what brings us joy. God put those things within us for a reason.

✓ We win when we become comfortable with who God made us to be instead of trying to hide our true selves from other people.

✓ We win when we work toward wholeness. Small, positive changes can make us whole in ways we never expected.

✓ We win when we become our authentic selves; people are drawn to that.

✓ We win when we help other people experience God's love through us.

✓ We win when we offer people the love of Jesus, knowing he can bring wholeness to them too.

CHAPTER 8

Us-Schooling

TODD

There's a song with the title "Old Time Religion." It's a catchy song, but if you grew up in the South, you really know what old time religion is all about. Staying on the "straight and narrow" is a real thing, as real as any Main Street that runs through the middle of town.

In the South, the straight and narrow has dos and don'ts—and everyone knows them. Not so much now, but movies and playing cards used to be a don't. And dancing was, too, unless you were dancing in the spirit of the Lord. Most music was frowned on, unless it came from a hymnal or worship CD. And church kids especially had to act a certain way. They had to act respectfully, dress appropriately, and not get too crazy about things. Instead of looking at the unique way God made each person, it was easier to keep kids in check unanimously, lest they stray. Nobody meant any harm, but for church people it was often easier to make things "off limits" than to discern every little thing.

Being a pastor's kid, it seemed all eyes were on me as I sat in the front pew. Even now I feel the tension tightening my gut. *You better not do that*, the voice in my head scolds in a southern drawl. But I've learned to answer: *Is it wrong? In light of Scripture—and not the ladies with the beehive hair that sat in the row behind me as a child—is it really wrong?*

The seeds of warning were scattered by enough well-meaning people that they not only took root in my heart but also grew tall. For many years, they filled the landscape of how I looked at the world. I've weeded out a lot, but the thoughts quickly take root again, especially when it comes to raising kids.

With our kids, Brooke and I have tried a different approach. Inside the boundaries of God's Word, we let them be who they are. We were almost forced to go in this direction, because Eagan was our first child, and he's insanely talented and different. We learned by parenting him. We let him be who he was. And I think that's the best decision we made. He's super comfortable being who he is.

Sometimes people think churchgoers are supposed to live stuffy lives—like being too creative or having too much fun is wrong somehow. Instead, God calls us to live life abundantly. For me, when it comes to my kids, that means riding the roller coasters, wrestling with the boys on the floor, dancing with my daughters, and teaching my kids that living for God can be a joy.

BROOKE

In the South, people have very clear ideas of the roles we should all play. It's something I've always resisted to a certain degree, and it might show in my parenting. I haven't always gotten it right as a mom, but I've allowed my kids to be comfortable with who God created them to be; not putting them in a box of what society says they should be has allowed each child to bloom.

Our son Eagan didn't play ball or ride four-wheelers. He doesn't hunt. Instead, he was creative and artsy from the beginning. He paints and draws. He loves making costumes and sews his own puppets. He sculpts and makes videos. Every day, something he does blows me away.

One of my favorite memories of him is from when he was five. We were at the playground, and he'd dressed himself up as Willy Wonka. He fully created the outfit and was so excited about it, but all the other kids laughed at him. For a minute, my heart broke. But when Eagan saw them pointing and laughing, he smiled and didn't care. He was fully who he was, and that inspires me to this day.

After Asher, Shepard, Judah, and Olive, I felt the urge to have another baby. That's when we had Hosea, and Louie was a full-on surprise. Then, when I felt like God had settled my anxiety, I urged Todd to trust God with our fertility. We conceived Wilhelmina Jolene that month, and we call her Winnie. She's four now and total personality.

TODD

Each of my kids is unique. I enjoyed art as a child, but Eagan takes it to another level. He has dedication and patience for what I consider tedious things. If he builds something that takes eight thousand blue feathers, he will glue on every one.

Asher creates music, and he raps. He's even rapped at some of my concerts. Out of all our kids, Asher is the most social. He thrives around people and always has a dozen conversations going with his friends at one time over text. He's funny but caring. When Asher's gone on mission trips, I've often heard back from the leaders that he was the one who people were drawn to the most. Sitting around the table and chatting with homeless people come easily to him.

Asher has become more comfortable with himself as he's gotten older, and sometimes it amazes me to look at pictures of him and see how much he's grown. One of my favorite photos, though, is from when he was seven. We'd just brought Olive home, and it was our first Christmas photos with five kids. We were at Clarkco State Park, and when the photographer was doing individual photos, Asher climbed up onto a jungle gym and fell off. Right away we knew his arm was broken, but since we'd already paid for the photo shoot we stayed and finished it. I'll blame the fact that we stayed on Brooke, but Asher was a trooper.

That's better, I suppose, than what happened to Shepard. His arm was broken for three days before we realized it. We thought if he could move it, he was fine. What we didn't realize was that he could move it, but he couldn't twist it . . . and it wasn't fine.

Shepard was the youngest of three boys in a row, and when he was little, he called himself the Hot Bobo. He came up with that himself. He had a mohawk and rode a kid motorcycle. He would make up dances, and he was the life of the party. As he's grown older, the Hot Bobo has become dependable and thoughtful. He's the one who says thank you for the little things like dinner or a burger out.

Shep likes gaming, graphic design, and computer stuff. He's not a social butterfly; he's a straight talker. He's the one Brooke and I can usually count on to do the right thing. But if he doesn't want to hang out with you, he won't hang out with you. And out of all the kids, Shep's the one who's most likely to come and talk with us without an agenda. He likes to hang out with Brooke and me just to hang out.

Judah is a typical girl, and she's social like Asher. She loves girl time with her best friend, taking selfies, and trying on outfits and shoes—especially now that she can fit into her mama's shoes. Judah has always been the dramatic one. Even when we first went and got her, she screamed and then gave me a look that could kill. I recently read a meme that said, "Anyone else grow up in a house where a loud sigh was considered 'talking back'?" Even if she's not saying it, she gets her point across. Yet she still loves sitting with me in my chair. I know she's outgrowing it, but I enjoy that she's a daddy's girl.

Olive likes doing some girly things too, such as doing her nails, especially with those big, gaudy fake ones. She also likes doing her hair. Mostly, Olive is a little helper and organizer, and she does a good job too. She's the one who keeps everyone in line—or at least tries. She knows the right way to do things, and she doesn't understand when the other kids don't listen to her. And Olive, more than anyone, keeps track of everything. She has inventory of our entire house. Whenever we don't know where something is, we ask Olive. She's a businesswoman, which I'm okay with. Recently, she offered to do all the laundry and named her price. I agreed. That girl's going someplace.

Hosea, at age eight, is Eagan 2.0. He's so much like Eagan that Brooke and I just look at each other in disbelief. He draws well, and he'll take the time to draw, paint, or put together a puzzle. He has the same drive in the creative direction as Eagan. He's also compassionate and sensitive, just like his oldest brother.

Louie is just the opposite of Hosea. He's as crazy, wild, and scattered as they come. Recently the church gave Hosea and Louie the same LEGO set. It was a big set made up of a lot of little projects. Before we even left the church, Louie's set was scattered, and we had no idea where the pieces were. Hosea, on the other hand, got up before anyone else the next morning and put together every one of those little kits.

Louie's just wild, and he's the mascot for adventure. He's the "take your shoes off, take your shirt off, and jump into the creek" type of kid. He always has stuff all over his face, and we always joke that he's a little bit feral. Yet every day he wants to sleep with Mama and Daddy. When I come in late from a concert and wanna curl up with Brooke, I'll end up curling up with Louie, who's curled up with Brooke. And last time this happened, I also ended up with my hand on the chewing gum that fell out of his mouth.

Louie's the one who will say, "I love you" out of nowhere. He's a scrapper and real defensive. If I'm messing around with Brooke like we're going to wrestle, he will come to Brooke's aid.

Winnie, who is four, is Brooke remade. She can be aloof at times and dramatic at other times. If I want to give Winnie a hug, she might give me one, or she might just roll her eyes and walk away. She loves on me . . . when she wants to.

Winnie is the typical baby of a large family. She is way too smart for her own good and way too sassy. When she wants something, she wants it now. Brooke's that way. When Brooke wants something from the store, she'll just jump in the car. It's not something to put on the list for later.

When we were doing the finale for *The Voice*, we'd already had the kids' wardrobe approved and ready to go. But Winnie didn't like how every time she raised her arms her shirt would go up and show her belly a little. We had to get back online for wardrobe, and Winnie wore a new outfit. I just smile at that kid, seeing so many of the qualities that made me fall in love with Brooke, stubborn streak and all.

BROOKE

I know that most of our kids are still young, and their unique gifts and talents are developing. I also know that allowing them to be who they are brings challenges. People—especially other kids— like everyone else to fit into a box. They are quick to point out when some kids are different, and sometimes in not-nice ways.

Because of his uniqueness, Eagan was bullied at school. Seeing his struggle, we decided to homeschool, and soon we brought all the kids home for their education. At first I thought, as a home-schooling mom, that things had to be done a certain way. But I soon realized that the greatest success comes when we just help shape our kids into who God has already created them to be.

Our kids' education might be different from what people expect, because we let them be individuals within their educa-tion too. Much of the kids' learning happens by living and doing life together. I like to call it "us-schooling."

This schooling choice has taught us to be authentic with our kids and to quit living our stories for other people. Todd and I know it's important for us to live a great story, and we allow our kids to do the same.

Us-schooling is about building a strong relationship between parents and kids. It's also about seeing our kids build special relationships with one another. We enjoy seeing our kids work together. We love seeing our older kids teach their younger siblings things they enjoy.

God called me to homeschool for the relational side. Nobody can love my children as I can. God's given me the opportunity to do it, so I'm going to do it. I love being with my kids. I have so many wonderful moments with them throughout the day. If they were at school, I would miss those conversations. The schooling stuff is a bonus.

We do life together—learning together, reading together, cooking together, playing together, praying together. I make sure my kids get reading, writing, and arithmetic basics down. And for the rest of it, we have fun exploring interesting subjects together.

"Together" for us means supporting one another's dreams too. Our kids have a front-view seat to see what Todd and I are doing, the risks we're taking as we follow God. They not only saw that their dad was willing to step out and do something crazy like try out for *The Voice*, but they also got to be a part of it when the production came home. They would have missed a lot of the hands-on experience if they had been away at school all day.

TODD

While we want our kids to discover their unique identities and learn, we also want them to know the beauty of family and "together."

One of the most common questions I get asked is: "What's the deal with that red string on your wrist?" When I'm asked that question, it gives me the opportunity to share how we are all united even when we're apart. It's a simple red piece of twine that I wear every day. So does Brooke. And so do the kids. It came from a time when we were going through a battle and needed to know that we were all in it together.

I won't go into details about what was happening, but now and then hell just kind of shows up at your door. That happened in our family a couple of years ago. We were angry and devastated and confused and pretty scattered. In the middle of that, Brooke suggested we use a spool of red twine from the kitchen drawer and make bracelets for each member of our family. All ten of us. We pulled it out, cut the lengths, and tied them on.

The red string reminds us that we don't fight alone. No matter where we are or what we face, we are always connected to people who are unwaveringly in our corner. All of us stand for any one of us, and any one of us stands for us all.

God saw us through that hard time, and we know he'll see us through more. We still have the spool, and we still clip off a new bracelet now and then. When a kid outgrows one or finds some creative way to destroy it, we tie another one on. I figure there's enough twine on that spool to last my lifetime, at least.

Each time we look at those red strings on our wrists and remember "together," we win.

WINS FOR TODAY

✓ We win when we look at each kid and discover who God created them uniquely to be.

✓ We win when we allow our kids to be comfortable with who they are.

✓ We win when we live a great story and allow our kids to do the same.

✓ We win when we teach our kids the importance of "together."

CHAPTER 9

Going Viral

BROOKE

As wonderful as Eagan's creativity is, when he faced a hard time in his life, his artwork reflected it. Eagan was bullied and hurt by many people, some of whom he'd trusted. It led to a place of deep depression. It was a tough season for him, and Todd and I struggled with how to help. For a while, Eagan was attracted to villain characters in his art; they're more layered. His art helped him to escape from the hard stuff, but Todd and I knew he still had to find peace on the inside too.

TODD

With my wife and kids, I feel this great responsibility to make sure everything's okay. I'm a peaceful pragmatic, and I knew things weren't right with Eagan. Always comfortable in his own skin, he began to struggle with how people treated him. People who used to be his friends lashed out at him, and I could see their words and actions piercing his heart.

The vast majority of people in our lives, and Eagan's life, have been good. But the handful who are not good sometimes can be *really* not good.

Eagan's art was taking a darker turn, and we didn't think much of it at the time. One day, however, he came home from work, and when I saw his downcast eyes, I knew something was wrong. At the time we lived in a house with a sunken living room, and he sat down on the step and just started to cry. He told us he just wanted to be a kid again—that he didn't want to grow up, that he just wanted to go back and be a kid.

Sometimes I'm so quick to try to fix things that it makes things worse, not better. I tried to tell Eagan, very practically, that he couldn't go back to being a kid. I tried to explain that each of us had to grow up, and that growing up is hard. But deep down I knew there was more going on than just a bad day at work. And there were other changes too.

Eagan is usually loud and passionate about the things he enjoys, but instead of this outward creativity, he started withdrawing to his room alone. Teenagers often do that, but this wasn't typical. My gut tightened with anxiety and fear, not knowing how I could help my son. Sometimes I'd lay awake at night worrying, wondering what was really going on. I'd ask myself as I tossed and turned: *Will he ever get past whatever this is?*

Sometimes, just to ease my mind, I'd ask him, "How are you doing?" hoping that everything would be okay.

"I feel good," he'd answer some days, and on those days, I felt the freedom to just breathe. I'd allow the worries to slip to the back of my mind for a while. But on other days, when he wasn't okay, the knot would tighten up in my gut again. And I could tell from the look on Brooke's face that she was worried too.

"It'll be okay. It always works out. We'll get through this," I'd tell her, wishing I believed my words.

Brooke suggested Eagan go to counseling. She also suggested

we gather people together to pray for our son. Finally, I decided to talk to Eagan about it—to ask what he thought he needed.

I remember sitting on the front porch with Eagan and him looking so lost. Even though he was now my size, I could see a hurt little boy in his eyes.

"What do you need me to do? How can I help you, son?" I asked.

"Maybe if I could just talk to the counselor at my school."

"Yes, of course."

Yes, we prayed for our son, and we will always continue to pray, but sometimes our kids need to see us act too. Looking back, sometimes the wins come when we don't have the answers. A win isn't always getting it right or figuring out the answers ourselves. Wins can be asking our kids what they need and listening.

Eagan seemed to find encouragement knowing that he was going to get the help he needed. The counselor ended up being a wonderful resource for him. She was invaluable to Brooke and me too. Even then, Eagan's depression reached a breaking point, and he needed more help than we could give. The hardest thing I've ever done in my life was leaving him in a facility to get help for ten days.

When Eagan returned home, he started doing better. It helped him to pour himself into his creativity, and one of the things he loved was dressing up his younger siblings in costumes. They loved it too. He'd dress up our youngest kids to look like Dorothy, the Tin Man, and the Cowardly Lion. There were also costumes of Moana, Jack Sparrow, Pebbles and Bamm-Bamm, Barbie, the Lost Boys, Edward Scissorhands, and so many more.

Eagan's imagination was kindled by movie and comic-book characters. He'd snap photos of the kids in his costumes and post them online, and everyone would be blown away. He created the costumes out of whatever was on hand, and they were elaborate. Since Eagan was little, he was drawn to the movies that Brooke and I watched growing up, like *E.T.*, *The Karate Kid*, *Labyrinth*, and *Star Wars*. He especially loved vintage movies and books. Once he even dressed up his siblings as the characters from his favorite movie *The Outsiders*. He's always loved Jim Henson and the Muppets the best, and so some of his favorite Muppet characters were represented in his costumes too. And just the other day, he dressed up his sister Winnie like a princess.

One day, when he was just seventeen, Eagan chose to dress up three-year-old Louie as Pennywise. Eagan liked the costume, and he asked Louie about it. Obviously, Louie said yes. If you're not familiar with Pennywise, it's a clown from Stephen King's horror novel *It*, which was also a recent blockbuster movie. Of course, Louie didn't know that. He just knew he was going to be a clown. He also couldn't see his own makeup, so it wasn't scary to him. Like with all the other costumes, Eagan made Pennywise from things he found around the house. He cut up old clothes and made the clown collar from an upside-down dress.

Louie thought it was fun posing. Eagan would tell him to do his happy face and then his mean face, and Eagan took the shots. When he posted them, those photos went viral. Popular culture sites talked about how Eagan's portrayal of Pennywise was nightmarishly realistic, especially considering he'd dressed a three-year-old in a chilling costume as a twisted clown. For us, Eagan dressing up his siblings like fictional characters was just what he did, but the response was unlike anything we'd ever seen or expected.

The movie's director, Andy Muschietti, liked the photo on Eagan's Instagram account. At the same time, hits on Brooke's Facebook page reached one hundred thousand likes in one day. Sites such as CinemaBlend, Cosmopolitan, and Bored Panda featured Eagan's photos, praising them. Eagan was just a teenager, and these big publications started asking him for interviews.

Of course, when something's getting that much attention, you can't keep it from the religious crowd. Right away we started receiving a lot of comments about how we'd allowed our older son to dress up our youngest son as a clown from a horror film.

First off, we didn't "allow" it. Eagan was always having fun with his little brothers and sisters, dressing them up and doing photo shoots with them. Then again, if he had asked, I'm not sure I would have told him no. It's not as if we were approving evil. In my mind and Brooke's mind, it was something fun that the kids did, and it was part of Eagan's artistic expression. But, of course, that's not how others saw it.

Even though Brooke and I knew that Louie didn't connect the dress-up to a movie, we were slammed by people's opinions. Some folks said they couldn't believe I'd preached all these years about doing what was good but then had seemingly gone and done the opposite, glorifying evil and presumably making money off it.

No one got any money. People were sharing Eagan's photos because this new movie was coming out, and our son did an excellent job. It wasn't glorifying evil, and I was happy that Eagan's talents were being appreciated. After going through such a hard time, he had something to be excited about. People praised his artistic talents, and what we were seeing in Eagan was positive and good. The positive reinforcement encouraged him. He was happy. I smiled seeing his smile again.

Yet Brooke and I also had to deal with the backlash. Even though I'd been a people pleaser for so much of my life, I chose to celebrate with my son. I told myself, *I'm not listening to this*, and blocked a lot of the comments on social media.

Facing the criticisms gave Brooke and me a good opportunity to really become clear on what we believe and how we ought to live. We believe that people do sin, but that's what Jesus's sacrifice was all about—to pay the price for that sin.

We also believe that God's plan had to do with more than just getting us into heaven. Like I said before, I don't think God sent his only Son to be born in a stable and live the life he lived—doing all the miracles, loving so many people, and then dying on the cross—just to keep us out of hell.

I think God did all that so we could know him, because he loves us and wants a relationship with us. We shouldn't just turn to Jesus to get into heaven or because we're scared of the alternative. Instead, as Jesus said very plainly: "The thief comes only to steal and kill and destroy. I came that they may have life and have it abundantly" (John 10:10 ESV).

The closer we get to Jesus, the more abundance we find. The closer we get to Jesus, the more we want to do the right things. Yet we also realize the things that at first might appear to be questionable are actually blessings in disguise. This was the case with Eagan.

So many people who commented and sent us messages were focused on the scary clown, while we were like, "Wow, look at all these people celebrating our son's talents. What an encouragement after this hard, hard season."

I've learned that when we're too focused on doing the right things—or not doing the wrong things—the focus is on us. We're actually making ourselves the center when Jesus should be the center. Jesus is supposed to be in the middle. Maybe abundant life isn't so much about how I respond to something that looks like it might be sin but instead how I respond to Jesus.

Looking back, we can see that Eagan's viral photos actually played a part in preparing us for *The Voice*, because when I got to the NBC stage, we heard from many people who believed a pastor should not be singing secular songs on national television. Again, we found ourselves getting lots of comments on social media.

We're learning that with whatever larger platform we have, the comments from those who don't like what we're doing will come. And I understand. Judging is easier than trusting. We often see just part of the story and fill in preconceived ideas.

I may not have done everything right with Eagan. I've told him a whole lot of times that we grew up *together*. When he was born, I was twenty-one. Still, I'm trying to do the best I can by talking to him. And more than that—listening. I want my kids to know that I appreciate them for who they are, and that it's okay if there are those who won't always understand or agree. And, honestly, I think I've been able to model that. I am doing what I feel God is asking me to do.

Dealing with Eagan—and all my kids—I can see how things have changed within me too. When I was growing up, a lot of the old tradition had to do with looking forward to heaven. I appreciate that what I learned in church helped me to long for the "sweet by and by." But as I've become an adult, I can now see there's a lot more that Jesus is doing in the here and now.

Brooke and I talk about always feeling as if we were on the

edge of our salvation, certain that if we did wrong too often we'd miss out on heaven. Being a father myself, I now understand unconditional love more than I ever have. All those years when I was so focused on doing right actually reflected a lack of faith and understanding of the love of my heavenly Father.

So when Eagan's work went viral, I wanted that to be a validation for him. And it wasn't just a whole bunch of ordinary people who were giving him praise. One group of people who reached out to him was a special effects team from the movie business. These were professionals who'd worked on many top films, including *Predator*. They knew the business, and Eagan's work impressed them.

These people honored my son for what others had teased him about. To receive that sort of affirmation really spoke to his heart. I know the message that came through was this: not only is what you're doing worthwhile and good, but you're really special and creative. When they reached out to Eagan, they didn't just say, "Good job." They invited Eagan and Louie to Los Angeles as their guests, and I got to go along for the ride.

In Los Angeles with the special effects team, Eagan was in his element. As he talked with the team, they spoke a language I didn't understand, and Eagan's face radiated with happiness.

They gave Eagan a behind-the-scenes tour. They also had a few projects for him to do while he was there. The team topped it off by giving him credit to a store in Hollywood where they buy their supplies. The place was massive, with all the equipment and materials you'd need for special effects in the film, commercial, or music industry. Eagan explored the store for hours, while I mostly chased Louie around. Eagan spent every penny and was thrilled with all his new supplies.

BROOKE

Even though it wasn't easy getting all the negative comments, it was easy celebrating Eagan. Looking back to August 2017, I shared this on Facebook:

> Louie and Eagan's done gone viral. They interviewed Eagan and everything.
>
> ***** Disclaimer*** I know [Louie's costume] is scary, but my focus is on Eagan's artistic ability and how much attention it's garnered. I'm very proud for him. Louie loves dressing up for Eagan and isn't scared at ALL. He actually LOVES clowns.
>
> Remember that the same people who have done the bloody shooting scenes for action movies and makeup for scary movies also did the makeup for Jesus on the *Passion of the Christ*. It's a craft. And Eagan is anointed to create.[1]

While Todd and I allowed Eagan to enjoy the attention he got from the viral photos, it also gave us a good opportunity to talk to him about his choices. People did take notice of what he was drawing or creating, and some of the characters that interested him represented values that were opposite of his faith. We told him that he needed to start thinking about those things. We shared our thoughts, but we also allowed room for the Holy Spirit to speak to Eagan's heart, and now—from his own conviction—he's decided to dress up his siblings as more wholesome characters.

By allowing Eagan's creative nature to shine, other doors opened. Eagan—at age nineteen—was a "creator" on the TV show *Making It*, with executive producers and hosts Amy Poehler and

Nick Offerman. The show is a competition between craftspeople skilled in different media, and the winner receives $100,000. Each week, competitors are judged on two handmade projects: a "faster craft," made within three hours, and a more elaborate themed "master craft."

Eagan first heard about the tryouts for *Making It* from someone who followed him on Instagram. He filled out the application but had trouble uploading his samples. Thankfully, the casting director did her due diligence, and she checked out his work online. After that, things happened quickly. They wanted to see more samples of his work, and Eagan went through lots of steps. It was nerve-racking as we waited to hear if he was on the show.

When Eagan finally emailed them to see if they'd made a decision, they got back to him to say that he hadn't made it and to try again next year. He was bummed, so I offered to take him thrifting, which he loves. Then he got the call that they'd changed their minds. He was in.

Eagan's crafting skills were displayed on broadcast television on a national level. In week one, for the faster craft challenge, the ten makers had to create a 3D presentation of a food that reflected who they were; for the master craft, they had to create a new version of their favorite childhood craft, showing how they've grown.

For the faster craft, Eagan made an Asian noodle box puppet to celebrate his sisters from South Korea, and he won. Eagan stayed in the competition through episode five. Throughout the show, he shared about his family. "We just tell people to look for the house with the kids running around with their underwear outside," he said, which is totally true.[2]

It also made my mama heart proud to hear him talk about

how Todd and I have always believed in his dreams. "I know not a lot of people live in households where their dreams are fully supported. But in our household, there's always been a very open policy of being who you are and doing what you love. You don't have to be a doctor or a lawyer just because that's the financially stable thing to do."[3]

Eagan also had a chance to talk about bullying. He shared how people used to tease him for being different, but he told them he's thankful that he didn't let that stop him from being who he was. As Eagan talked about bullying, it really struck a chord with one of the other makers, Floyd. That was my favorite part of the show, for Eagan to share his story and for it to connect with someone else on a deep level. And I know if his story helped Floyd that it no doubt helped countless others.

I love how God was able to have more amazing people applaud Eagan's work without crushing his creativity. On *Making It*, Eagan was able to authentically share himself. Even after Eagan was eliminated, Nick Offerman brought a smile to my face when he said, "Which one of us is calling Eagan's mom to tell her he's not coming home?"[4]

Eagan was loved by everyone there, and people were amazed at his creativity and poise at such a young age. It was hard having him gone for a whole month, but he really showed us that his work is worthy of being appreciated at a national level.

Also, when Todd first auditioned for *The Voice*, Eagan had just been doing his thing with NBC. Eagan had finished filming *Making It* in April 2019, and Todd tried out for *The Voice* just months later. We didn't even realize that *The Voice* was on the same network. It's not like we had an in with NBC or anything. Both of these events were completely random. But I did use Eagan's leap of faith to encourage Todd. I told him, "Todd, you always tell Eagan to do what he loves and pursue what he loves. Why don't you just try that?"

In a strange way, God has somehow given us a voice in the media world. It doesn't make any sense other than that we just felt called to explore these gifts he's given us and to take these leaps of faith. And somehow that ended up being part of God's big plan. We're willing to be hope and light to people, we're willing to be authentic, and God is using that. People can spot fake right away. They can see that we're willing to share our low spots as well as our victories, our losses with our wins.

———— • ————

Not everyone is gonna be happy about you achieving your dreams, especially if they don't think you're doing everything just like they think you should. Again, we had to find freedom from what the church culture thought we should be doing and be fully who God created us to be, while also honoring him the best we could.

It's been important for us to quit living our stories for what others think is acceptable. It's also been important for us to allow our kids the same freedom to live their great stories. Along the way they will make mistakes; all of us do. They can learn from that too. And we—as parents—can help them.

It would be nice if we could say that, as parents, we always do everything right, but it's not that easy. Sometimes what helps one kid won't help the other one. Sometimes we really mess up. This happened with our son Shepard.

He is the youngest of our three oldest boys and he was always the smallest. He also had to have eye surgery and he has a kidney issue. Because he was so tiny, I'd always joke around and tell people he was the runt of the litter. I thought it was cute; everyone loves the sweet little one. But a couple of years ago, Shep told me that it bothered him. It made him feel less than. I felt horrible to have hurt his feelings so many times. Even though I thought it was sweet, I had to listen to him. I apologized and asked him to forgive me. Seeking forgiveness is also a win.

We can be active in our children's lives, and that's a win. We can pray about what's going on, and that's a win too. We win when we seek God's Word. We win when we share what's on our hearts with our kids, and hopefully our kids will learn how to be transparent with us in return.

We win when we do what we can and trust that God will speak to our kids' hearts too. And we know that even when things seem impossible, following God is always a win.

WINS FOR TODAY

✓ We win when we confess our mistakes as parents.
✓ We win when we fight for our kids when things get hard.
✓ We win when we make ourselves available to help and support our kids.
✓ We win when we find others who can help in ways we can't. Sometimes a counselor, teacher, or coach can be a lifeline for our kids.

✓ We win when we celebrate what our kids are doing well, even when we see other areas where they're struggling.

✓ We win when we ask our kids, "How can I help you?"

✓ We win when we talk with our kids and listen.

✓ We win when we teach our kids to follow God's ways above all else.

CHAPTER 10

The Goodness of God

BROOKE

Living on a pastor's small salary has taken faith, especially as our family has grown. We've relied on the goodness of God. We've never had a savings account. We've always lived paycheck to paycheck. Yet we've found some good in that too. For example, I love thrifting and resale. Through that, God has enabled us to take care of our large tribe. God has always provided, and our kids have always been dressed cute on thrift-store purchases.

I love the experience of getting the deal. It's a thrill to get something that I know costs a lot for cheap. Not spending a lot of money was ingrained in me when I was young. It continued as I got married. But honestly, I think God has honored our leap of faith to enlarge our family, especially when we technically didn't have money to support all the kids. God has always been faithful. He's provided the money for the adoptions, and thrifting is one of the ways God uses to provide for us on a daily basis.

I bet that 97 to 98 percent of the clothes we wear are thrift store purchases. Of the stuff in our house, 95 percent is thrift or resale. Thrifting is therapy for me. I can't imagine not doing it. And I feel as if God really shows up to meet my needs. If one of the kids needs something particular, I'll find that exact thing within a few days. I may even find something that one of the other kids wants.

For example, one of my kids wanted to learn guitar, and we didn't have one. Not a week later there was a guitar at the Salvation Army. And there's no way I could go buy eight Easter or Christmas outfits, so I've learned the knack of buying ahead. I also know there are certain shoes I'll always grab, like Converse— they're always in style, and they're gender neutral. So if I see them, and they're in good shape, I pick them up, even if they're not the size my kids are wearing yet.

I have a system. I know which thrift stores have the best kids' clothes and which ones have the best shoes. I've learned to go on a regular basis, and I know where to look for the items that are just put out. I always want my kids to look cute.

Thrifting even saved the day when Todd was on *The Voice*. With production coming home, we were doing everything ourselves. We were so stressed. We hadn't washed clothes, and I needed specific clothes without any logos or pictures for my kids, since all of them were going to be in the live filming for Todd's song "Love, Me."

I went to a store called Dirt Cheap, which sells retail clothes highly discounted. I got everything for those video shoots off the two-dollar rack. God takes care of us in that way. And, yes, my kids did look cute in front of over seven million viewers.

TODD

Even after I won *The Voice*, Brooke chose to thrift shop as she has always done through seasons when we honestly didn't have an extra penny. Holidays were especially tough. Our older kids would joke about some of their Christmas gifts from times past.

"Remember when Santa brought us Dad's old Xbox?" they'd say, recalling some of those very lean Christmas days. They remember getting gifts they were pretty sure came from thrift shops, yet the joy of the celebration overshadowed that.

Also, Brooke almost gets a high from buying something great at a discount. She even makes me pick up stuff that people have put on the curb. It's a big deal to her. She takes joy in telling others how God has provided again and again.

With a big family, we've learned that we don't have to spend a lot on meat. We can do a lot with rice and noodles. And then there are unexpected blessings that drop into our laps. For example, we recently got a call from someone who had bought a brand-new mattress. They had it a week, and they didn't like it. Instead of just taking it back, they asked us if we wanted to come by and get it. We're still sleeping on it, and it's great. Those kinds of things have happened. And just as people have been generous to us, we try to do the same. But we've found we can't out-give God.

When we've had the opportunity to be generous, inevitably somebody would bring us a freezer full of deer meat or some cartons of eggs or some vegetables from their garden. We've gotten calls that people have gone fishing and want to drop some of the filets by our house. Our freezer and pantry, for the most part, stay well stocked just from stuff people give us. A lot of times we've probably made the wrong decisions financially, but God was still faithful.

We are never in want. God has shown us that he is a generous God. And realizing that is a win.

———◆———

I have one son who's especially good at asking for things he needs. He likes to record music, and sometimes he may need a piece of equipment or something. He knows what he wants, and he will keep asking because he trusts that eventually his daddy is going to take care of it. You know, we have a large family, which means I can't always buy every piece of equipment he wants—but he knows that when I *can* do it, I *will* do it.

Too often, when things are hard, we perceive that God only gives us what we deserve. If that's the case, we're all in trouble. Instead, God cares for us like a good father does a son. One scripture says, "You parents—if your children ask for a loaf of bread, do you give them a stone instead? . . . So if you sinful people know how to give good gifts to your children, how much more will your heavenly Father give good gifts to those who ask him" (Matt. 7:9, 11 NLT).

I'm in awe as I see where I am now, knowing that all of this came from God's good gifts for me. Even though we're just in the gestational stages of this new move into music, there is a whole lot of hope for the future, and a whole lot more freedom too.

That scripture from Matthew speaks to my heart in relatable ways. My kids have made me the proudest man on earth. Every one of them at different times, in different ways, for different reasons. But do you know what? There are other times when my kids have disappointed me. They've disobeyed me.

But it doesn't matter how many times they disobey; I will still never give them a stone. Even if I'm upset, even if I'm outright angry or disappointed or frustrated, whether they do things that make my heart sad or glad, there has never been a time when, if my children asked me for bread, I would give them a stone. And this is the goodness of God.

Sometimes when it appears that God has given us a stone, it actually ends up being bread. Looking back at our marriage struggles, we see that we overcame—and our marriage was bread to us. We thought Brooke's anxiety and depression were stones, but seeing God's faithfulness, we know now that season was bread. She grew from that experience, and she's helping others. We even see that the struggles with our children are bread because in our weakness, we turn to God again and again. And in our lack, God has shown himself abundant. Bread indeed.

The gospel has never been about how bad we are. Maybe that's something you grew up learning from church or church people, or, maybe, like me, that's just how you perceived things. The gospel is always about how good God is. Always, always, always. So we shouldn't refrain from going to the Father and asking and seeking and knocking, because he loves us—each of us. And we can trust that what he gives us will be bread, even when it doesn't seem like it at the time.

I'm not trying to say we don't need to change our lives. I think every one of us needs to change our lives. But I don't think very many of us can just will ourselves to change. In my growing-up years, change happened to me as I sang. Even though I'd repeated the same lyrics and sang the same familiar chords for years, it wasn't until I leaned in to God—and stopped worrying so much about getting it all right—that my singing made me different inside. We all have to rely on the goodness of God. He is good. He provides in amazing ways.

If anybody told me I could use only one word for the rest of my life to describe God, I would choose this: *good*. Things weren't perfect when I was a kid, even though I was raised in the church. Things were far, far from perfect for the many years I pastored. And even since winning *The Voice*, things still aren't perfect. But God is. He has always provided for us, and he always will. He gives us bread, even though it may not seem like it at the time. And finally understanding this is a win.

WINS FOR TODAY

✓ We win when we understand that God knows our needs and even our wants.

✓ We win when we find joy in telling others what God has provided for us.

✓ We win when we understand that we can't out-give God.

✓ We win when we're generous with the little that we have.

✓ We win when we think God has given us a stone, but instead we see bread.

CHAPTER 11

Road to *The Voice*

TODD

It was a four-and-a-half-hour drive to the open call auditions in Atlanta, Georgia, and at least a hundred times along the way I wondered why I was taking the time to do this. I kept thinking, *If it wasn't for Brooke's persistence, I could be home right now relaxing or wrestling with my kids.* Yet I knew if I said no, I'd never hear the end of it. There's a verse in Proverbs that says, "A nagging wife is like water going drip-drip-drip on a rainy day" (27:15 GNT). And that's the truth when it comes to Brooke.

"Todd," she told me with hands on her hips, "you have to go. If you don't, you'll never know. If you don't, you'll always wonder. If you don't, you might regret it." *Drip, drip, drip.*

It's not that I didn't think I could sing. It's just that I didn't think I was what the casting directors at *The Voice* were looking for. I knew that *American Idol* doesn't even let you try out if you're over twenty-eight years old. I assumed that the people from *The Voice* were looking for someone young, beautiful, and talented. And I was one of the three. Maybe.

Years prior, on an anniversary trip, Brooke and I discovered tryouts were happening for *America's Got Talent*. I tried out just for fun, and they seemed very interested, but they never called me back. After that, in my time of discontent, I thought maybe it would be a good idea to try to do more with music. I started teaching myself piano. I tried guitar too, but I didn't go far with either.

The journey to *The Voice* started when an acquaintance emailed me information about an open call in Atlanta. I went online and reserved a spot, but I didn't receive an email confirmation. I wasn't sure my application went through, and I actually forgot about it.

The week prior to the audition, Brooke had a conference in Colorado. She's directionally challenged, and I thought it would be nice to get away for a while, so I decided to drive her there. I enjoyed a few days alone in a cabin, spending time with God and hiking around. I didn't think about the audition until we got home, and then Brooke and I remembered that it was the next day.

I still wasn't sure if I really had a spot in the open audition. But when I went online and saw the confirmation, Brooke insisted that I go. (*Drip.*) I was annoyed as I packed an overnight bag. Since we'd just gotten back from Colorado and didn't have any extra money, my plan was to drive to Atlanta and sleep in my car, then head into the audition the next morning.

I'd almost gotten to Atlanta when I got a call from a church member. "Pastor Todd, we can't have our pastor sleeping in the car," he said. "Get a hotel, and we'll take care of it." I relented and found the cheapest hotel I could. I got up at about four thirty in the morning and dressed in a pair of khaki shorts, a T-shirt, and some sandals. Then, with a jumble of butterflies in my stomach, I drove to the location.

When I got downtown, where the audition was, I had to pay twenty-five dollars to park. That frustrated me because we had almost zero money, but I had no choice but to pay it.

The line looked as if it wrapped around the block, and it did. But it not only wrapped around the block, as the line moved on, it zigzagged through a parking garage, into the building, through the building, and then up some steps. It was insane. And the whole time I was really frustrated because it seemed like a total waste of my time and money. I'd known there would be a lot of people, but I'd had no idea the line would be *that* long.

I stood in line for hours. Dozens and dozens of people were practicing around me, and they all sounded good. Every now and then there would be security checks, making sure we were all supposed to be there.

As I finally reached the front of the line, I watched as groups of people entered the casting room and then exited disappointed. I told myself that no matter what happened, at least I was here. At least I tried.

In my heart, my intimidation level was through the roof. When I finally got to the section where we were divided into small groups, I sat in a chair overwhelmed with it all. I legitimately sat there with my head down, elbows on my knees, just waiting. Waiting to sing. Waiting to go home. Waiting to get back and tell Brooke, "There, I tried."

The entire time I was sitting there, a woman to my left was preaching to all of us about how there was no chance we were getting through the open call. She told us that the chances of any of us making it through this audition were one in a million. I'm not sure why she was saying that, but it didn't help me. And then to see disappointed face after disappointed face leaving the building didn't help either.

When I finally got my chance to sing, a rush of excitement flowed through me. The drive no longer seemed to matter. The wait didn't either. A surge of joy filled me knowing that now was my chance to sing, which I love to do. I suppose there was a little win in the middle of all of that.

There was no music, so I started just a smidge higher than I would have, but either way it turned out okay. With a smile, I stood in front of the casting team and sang thirty seconds of "Broken Halos" by Chris Stapleton.

I had gone into the audition room with a group, and when we were all finished, the casting director thanked everyone for coming. Then, to my surprise, she asked a few of us to stick around. Without giving specifics, I was invited back the next day to audition further.

My mind was spinning, and I called Brooke first. Her squeals filled the air. Then I had to call one of the church leaders to ask him to fill in since I was supposed to preach the next day. He eagerly agreed and told me he'd be praying.

In the morning, instead of heading back to Mississippi, I ran to a store to buy another outfit. I'd only packed one, and I was wearing it. Then I went back to the hotel, downloaded additional songs, and tried to practice the best I could without waking anyone up. I added "We've Got Tonight" by Bob Seger to the songs I wanted to sing. Brooke had recommended that I sing it, and I liked that song.

When I got to the audition, they asked me to sing. I did, belting out "We've Got Tonight." I could tell they were all happy. They were looking at and elbowing one another. When I finished, the casting director nodded, then asked, "Okay, well, what do you want to do next?"

"You want me to do more?" I couldn't believe it. "Okay, I'll do whichever song. You pick one."

"No, you tell me," the woman answered with a smile.

"Well, let's just do 'Broken Halos.'"

Then they asked me to sing my third song. I took that as a good sign. They seemed pleased—whoever they were.

To this day, I don't know all the people who were there, but I sang "Brown Eyed Girl" next. The funny story is that when I got near the end of the song—to the very last verse—I blanked. I could not remember the words. I mean, the words were seriously not coming. But God saved my butt. The woman with my phone just turned the track off right there. And she was like, "Oh, that's good, thank you."

I released a huge sigh of relief. *Thank you, God.*

They also recorded interviews. One of those interviews is still up on Instagram on *The Voice* casting page: "I'm just a straight-up Mississippi boy, like all the way, hard core. I'm country come to town over here. I don't really hunt or fish, though, but I do love the outdoors. And my wife is not barefoot and pregnant, even though she has been pregnant a lot of times. When we got married, my wife said she wanted three kids, and I said I wanted two kids. And so we always tell everyone we compromised and had eight."[1]

The casting crew then talked about the show. I knew there were always four coaches and that if more than one coach turned, you got to pick who you wanted to be your coach. And if some miracle happened, and all four turned, then you got to pick one from the four. With a smile, someone from casting asked who I would pick if I were ever in that position.

"I would pick Blake for sure. Number one because, that's like today they were all like, 'try the same genre,' but I don't really do one genre. You know, I do all these different things. But I'm just a deep South boy to the core, and so I feel like that would probably be the best thing."[2]

The casting crew told me that if I made it further, I'd get a call. I went back home to Mississippi to my family and my normal life, and then the waiting came. As July slipped into August, I wondered each day if I'd get a call. The days passed, and I tried to just forget about it. Still, a small bit of hope was hidden in my heart. When the call finally came, my heart hammered in my chest. I'd been invited to Los Angeles for further casting for *The Voice*. This was really happening.

The casting directors let me know up front that at this level, hundreds of people were invited to come, and from there, some of the singers would be chosen to go further. I had no idea if I'd get a chance to audition on the actual show. I knew they were still considering so many great singers, and there were very, very few who would actually get a shot to sing before the coaches. Still, it was more than I ever imagined. This country boy was really going to town now.

An LA sound stage isn't typically where you'd find a Mississippi pastor, yet I soon discovered that people are people. I found joy in getting to know the other contestants and the staff working on the show. Each day was a new adventure. I enjoyed every moment of being there—singing and listening to amazing songs. I loved seeing how things worked behind the scenes. Just having the chance to get a glimpse of this different world thrilled my heart, and to know that my family and church were at home cheering me on and praying for me meant everything. They believed in me, and they were all making sacrifices for me to get this shot. I was a blessed man.

I hoped that I could at least make it on the show. And then

from there it would be amazing to have one chair turn. I had no expectations of winning. In fact, I knew I wouldn't win. Some of the other contestants had large social media followings. Others were popular on YouTube, in viral videos, or at venues. Most of the musicians were used to being on the road and doing gigs. They were all semiprofessionals, or so it seemed to me. Each performance I gave before the casting directors and executives was like a series of little wins, one after the other.

In a strange way, in Los Angeles, I also felt fully myself, even though I was completely out of my comfort zone. I was free to enjoy music all day long. I was singing, and people who weren't just my family and friends were appreciating it. I was loving people and sharing very real conversations, and I felt God's favor as I did. It was exciting to see that God could use me here, just as he used me in Meridian.

On the last night of executive casting—before all of us flew home—a bunch of us potential contestants went to dinner. We had a big feast, and we talked about how exciting it was to even be considered at this level. Everyone was cutting up and joking, and they all called themselves "Todd's children" because I was so much older than all of them.

That night, as I laughed and joked around with all my new friends, I told them, "You know what, guys, I have a feeling that someone here at this table is going to win this thing." After I won, a few of them—some who made it onto the show and some who didn't—reminded me that I'd said that.

When the time came for the filmed audition before the coaches, Brooke and Eagan stood on the sidelines, watching from backstage. I was thankful they were able to come and be with me. I loved having them close, and the twinkle in Brooke's eyes declared: "See, I told you so." Yes, she'd been right. Like many other meaningful things in my life, she'd pushed me out of my comfort zone, and it had turned out for the good.

"There's no way we're gonna win," I told Brooke, just so she'd get a touch of reality. "But let's hope for one chair turn." That was my big dream.

The music started and the words came out. I attempted to focus on the song and not those chairs. And then, before I knew it, three turned almost at the same time: Kelly, Blake, and Nick. And not too long after, the fourth chair turned. John Legend's face came into view with a large smile.

I couldn't believe it as Nick Jonas stood, smiling, and looking to Kelly as he watched me sing. Even though I had practiced staging with the crew, all of that was out the door—out of my mind. As soon as those chairs turned, I bounced and moved, trying to contain my joy even as I continued to sing.

The song ended, but my bouncing didn't. Everyone in the audience was on their feet. All the coaches were too. I still can't believe that even now. Kelly Clarkson, Nick Jonas, John Legend, and Blake Shelton were on their feet, clapping for me. What in the world?

John Legend was waving four fingers in the air, noting the four-chair turn. My cheeks hurt from smiling, but I couldn't stop. Laughter spilled from my mouth. Four turns meant all four coaches wanted me on their teams. I went into my joy zone, for real. With excitement and gratitude, I couldn't keep my body still. I did a few hops and a few spins, unable to contain my excitement.

Finally, when things settled down, John asked for my name and where I was from.

"Todd Tilghman. I am forty-one years old, and I'm from Meridian, Mississippi."

"I need to know about you," John said.

"Most importantly, I am married for twenty-one years to my beautiful wife, Brooke. We have eight kids."

"*What?*" said Kelly.

"Two are adopted."

"Dear, Lord!" said John with his hands raised.

"I need y'all so bad. You don't even know. Like . . ."

Laughter filled the sound stage.

"I was the last one to turn, but once I turned, I just saw the joy and the spirit that you have," John said.

"I love it," I said, unable to hide my grin. "I've literally never performed. I just sing at church. I pastor a church."

The coaches seemed shocked that I was a pastor and had never performed professionally. John, Nick, and Kelly tried to win me over, sharing about growing up in church.

"My grandfather was our pastor," John told me. "My mother was the choir director. I was at church on Sunday morning, Sunday night, Wednesday night, sometimes Friday night."

Nick tried to one-up John by saying that his father was a pastor. He told me that his most fond memories were at the piano, singing praise and worship songs. He asked me if I knew Phillips, Craig & Dean, and we sang a verse of one of their songs together. "We can talk life, music—I don't have kids yet, but you could give me some advice there," Nick joked.

"Oh, I can tell you how," I told him, and everyone loved that.

Kelly, too, talked about singing in church, and she understood how it was hard to follow this type of dream with so many kids.

But when Blake talked, I really connected with what he said:

I love your voice. I love the passion. I love the range. I love how not smooth it is. It gives you something to get ahold of. And you got a great hop." He then labeled it a holy hop. "You are so amped up, and it reminds me why I continue to want to be a coach on this show is to work with people like you."[3]

When it came down to picking my coach, my mind fixed on Blake Shelton. I liked what he had to say, but I also liked that he was a bit older and had lived life and faced hard stuff, just like I had. I felt we had relatable personalities and could connect on different levels, even more than just music. I picked Blake, and I've never regretted that decision. The friendship that grew has meant a lot, and some days I'm still amazed that all of that really happened.

Watching that audition video, I love seeing Kelly tell John, "He's so excited." She said it more than once, and excitement is an understatement. In that moment, as I started singing, I didn't think of all the pain that Brooke and I have faced through the years. I didn't consider that we almost didn't survive as a couple. I also wasn't thinking specifically about answered prayer either; I was mostly just thankful. Thankful that as impossible as it was of me being there, it was happening. *This* was part of God's story for me.

On that stage, I hoped the coaches would like my singing, but I was equally celebrating just being there. Just me standing on that stage was a win enough. That moment wasn't a culminating moment. I wasn't trying to find my worth there. If no chair turned, I still had an amazing wife and family to go home to. I still had a community of friends. But I also knew that God *could* do the impossible if he chose to.

I had already won so many times in life as God pulled me

from the mud again and again. To have people enjoy my singing would simply be a bonus. Being there was enough. The freedom I found in that moment was a win.

On that stage, the joy of the moment—and the emotions of seeing the chairs turn—overwhelmed me, and I know that the coaches and the viewers were drawn to that. They were drawn to my smile and my body that couldn't hold in all that I was feeling. But I think they were also drawn to my surrender. I was enjoying it all and simply giving myself to the moment, because, why not?

That's not to say I didn't struggle leading up to this moment. When I was practicing for my blind audition, my vocal coach turned to me and asked, "Are you okay, Todd? You seem uptight."

"I guess I am," I told her. "All of these people are young and beautiful. Most of them have some type of musical career. They've traveled around. Some have been in musicals. Others have won awards. You know, all things I've never done."

But in that moment onstage none of that mattered. God had given me that moment, and that was more than most people got in a lifetime.

The next few weeks were equally unbelievable. I spent time with Blake, going over music. I spent lots of time with the other contestants, building friendships. And I was able to meet other amazing music artists.

I tried to pick songs that were either strong in story or strong in emotion. I knew that sometimes people focus on lines or runs in songs and miss the bigger story or emotions behind the words. I thought of the viewers, and I knew I was singing for them too.

During the battle rounds, I was paired against Jon Mullins, who had become a friend. I knew to prep for the rounds we would get help from our coach, Blake Shelton, and a celebrity coach. I was nervous as all get-out that I would get in there and not know who the celebrity coach was.

I strode in to see this beautiful young lady sitting next to Blake. I lifted my hands in greeting. "Bebe!" I called out with excitement. Yes, it was Bebe Rexha.

The song that Blake gave Jon and me was "Ghost in This House." It's a classic song that's sacred to hardcore country music fans, and I knew we'd be under a microscope when performing it. I told Blake and Bebe that I had high hopes for this time in Los Angeles, even though it was hard being away from my family.

"*The Voice* could change everything for me," I told them. "Right now, I only sing at church. I don't perform or record. And to be able to support my family strictly through music would be a dream."[4]

Even now, I'm surprised that I spoke those things out loud. But then again, I think that's why people connected with me. They saw my vulnerability.

When it came down to the battle, Jon and I did our best, and I know the coaches and viewers saw our hearts. The other coaches gave their input, but the decision came down to Blake, and he was hesitant.

"I made a monumental mistake by pairing you two together," he admitted, "and, Jon, that's really to your credit. You're the one that stepped up and made this into this impossible decision because it was such an epic performance."[5]

I held my breath as Blake declared me the winner, and then I grew excited when Nick Jonas used his "steal" to take Jon. Each coach has one opportunity to choose a singer that the other coach has let go. I was excited about Jon getting to work with Nick. I was excited for all my friends. I loved seeing them succeed.

When it came to meeting my "mega mentor" for the next round of battles, I didn't get any hints. The staff member told me I would know who it was, and I did. I walked in that room of the sound stage for practice, and seeing our mega mentor was like a dream. I got chills all over. I just remember running up on the sound stage and saying, "You've got a friend," referring to his popular song. I couldn't even say his name. James Taylor, the icon, was sitting before me.

Standing next to James Taylor, I told Blake, "I freakin' love James Taylor."[6] I was clearly unable to control my emotions.

Now, when I watch that video, I wish I would have paid closer attention to what was happening at that moment, because I was shoulder to shoulder with James Taylor who was trying to talk to me about my music. I was just too stunned to take it all in.

The most validating part of my time with James Taylor was actually the most humbling. It's like an oxymoron for that level of people to be validating my singing. Tears still fill my eyes when I think about James Taylor's words: "I just can't believe there are people like you in the world, and we just don't even know, like we don't even know that you exist." I'm pretty sure those words are one of the things I will never forget.

For the knockout round, I sang "Anymore" by Travis Tritt. I won that round, and I was set to move on in the competition, but then everything changed. As everyone knows, my season didn't go as planned. The pandemic hit our country and impacted everything. Right in the middle of the season, I found myself home without any idea of what was going to happen or if I'd get to sing before those coaches—or the viewers—again. And that's truly when I had to trust that God did have a good plan, even if it meant my dream being cut short.

———◆———

I don't love God more because he took me to *The Voice* stage, but deep, deep down I began to understand God's love in a new way, and I saw even more clearly that there was purpose in the pain. There was also purpose in the times I felt lost or afraid. There was purpose in all those hours of prayers for direction, all those times I was seeking him.

There was purpose in the hours and hours and hours of leading people in worship with exuberance or the equal number of hours standing and singing a hymn at the bedside of a lonely and hurting saint. Because all of that had come before, I was able to be fully myself during my performances, and that was a win. I was my full self because that's all I had to offer, and that's exactly what God asks of each of us.

It was also a win to trust God even when things looked as if they weren't going to turn out like I'd thought they would. A worldwide pandemic threatened dreams I never realized I had, and at that moment, I had to trust that God had a good plan for me right in the middle of it.

WINS FOR TODAY

✓ We win when we know that God can do the impossible.
✓ We win when we discover freedom in areas where we once felt held back.

✓ We win when we connect with others who celebrate who God has created us to be.

✓ We win when we realize that God is still good no matter what.

CHAPTER 12

Minor Disappointments, Major Victories

BROOKE

When Todd received a four-chair turn on *The Voice* and got so much encouragement from the coaches, I couldn't have been more excited. But as excited as I was for this opportunity for Todd, worries and anxiety filled my mind. I wanted the best for Todd, but I worried he'd get his hopes up and then something would happen. Since so many bad things had happened in the years prior, I expected that something would go wrong with his time on *The Voice* too.

Yet when I prayed about it, a strange peace came—something I wasn't used to. My spirit lifted with joy as a whisper of God's promise filtered in my heart: *Brooke, don't worry. The bad thing is not going to happen this time. Trust me.*

Todd was able to perform numerous times in Los Angeles, and he kept moving on in the competition when many others were eliminated. Then the coronavirus hit. I mean, how could anything good come out of that?

Everyone was sent home, and nearly a month passed. We didn't know if season 18 would end right then or if they'd just have to wait until filming started in Los Angeles again. There was a time when I wondered if there'd be a competition at all. I'll be honest, from my perspective, and I think from Todd's too, at first I was disappointed. It took a little time for the producers to figure it out. Everybody was having to learn as they went.

The first days after Todd was sent home, I was discouraged that he wasn't going to get the full experience. I remember thinking and praying, *God, you promised me that the bad thing wasn't going to happen. You promised me that this was going to be good.*

When I was praying, God impressed something in my spirit: *Brooke, if you look at this only through the lens of how it can benefit you, you're going to be disappointed, even if Todd wins the whole thing. But if you shift your perspective to what I want to do out of this and what I want to accomplish, you're not going to be disappointed no matter what. No matter how they decide to do it. No matter what happens.*

In that moment, I had to shift my perspective. I remembered that the word I was dedicating to my year was *gratitude*. At the beginning of 2020, God started putting that on my heart. And so I shifted my perspective to being grateful. Either way— whether the season continued or not—Todd's experience was a huge opportunity. I had to trust that God was gonna make good on whatever he wanted to do with it.

I didn't want Todd to be let down, but what happened was amazing. Within a month, production made this huge shift, and the show continued from home. I think God was laughing at me then because he knew the bigger picture. I don't know why I'm like a toddler and pitch a tantrum when things don't go my way; God has shown me that his plan is always perfect.

When production continued from home, it was like a Pelican case of equipment showed up at our house. There were pro cameras, props, lights. Every day I'd come home and there'd be four or five huge boxes delivered. And that's when the real fun began.

TODD

Our family has always been a team, and we all pitched in to make things happen. The producers wanted me to film from our house, but I knew my kids would be all over that equipment, so we set it up at the church. From there I sang "Glory of Love" by Peter Cetera. If you watch the video, you can see the church's drum set in the back.

I sang the song with emotion, even though I didn't have the coaches or the crowd there. Production was just faces on the screen. Still, I guess viewers connected with my singing. Millions of people watched, and lots of them were rooting for me and voted me on. I'm grateful for everyone who did.

I was nervous at the top 17, which was the next level of competition. I was nervous at the top 9, the level after that. Yet, at the finale, it's not that I wasn't nervous at all, but I had a certain peace. I'd made it further than I thought I would. I was literally the opposite of everything they say you need for a music career, yet there I was.

I was forty-two years old by then, and as the show continued, I began to understand that maybe this whole thing wasn't about what God was doing for *me*, but what God wanted to do for *the viewers*. In this crazy time in history, God had a plan to bring hope to people, and for some reason, he chose me to offer it.

The further I got into the show, the more I was blown away with the response. I thought about those I had sung to in nursing homes or in hospitals. When they were scared or lonely, I often didn't have the words, so I just sang; somehow that gave them hope. And now, the whole nation felt alone and scared, and all God asked me to do was sing. I did, trusting that people would feel the hope that God gave me and discover it was available for them too.

If no pandemic had happened, if *The Voice* had gone on as normal, would the viewers have gravitated toward me in the same way? I'm not sure. They not only listened and voted for me, they reached out to me online. They started tuning in to my virtual services at Cornerstone Church. They told me how much my joy meant to them. They asked me for prayer. Without the pandemic, my truest fans might have been curious and looked me up, but the fear and lack of hope drew thousands more to my Facebook page.

"God is wherever you are," I told those watching and commenting. I knew this meant not only physically but also emotionally. He was with me in Mississippi and with that grandmother in Salem, Oregon, who decided to turn off the television news and instead tune in to watch me talk on Facebook Live about Jesus. He was with our family as we tried our best to set up lights and props. And he was with the nurse who had to balance caring for a flood of COVID-19 patients while also caring for her kids at home.

I haven't been perfect in my life, but I've tried to be faithful. And God says that when we're faithful in the small things, he will give us bigger things. Whoever can be trusted with little can also be trusted with much.

God took me to the finale as viewers voted me through. Win or lose, I knew I'd made it. We'd made it.

Setting up for the finale was crazy, and the production crew loved Eagan because, even though they couldn't be there, they had someone on the ground to be creative. Brooke helped with the camera and all of that, but Eagan did the props. The producers trusted Eagan, and they gave him freedom to do what he thought looked good. With so much going on, he made it easier on them.

When I made it to the top 9, I performed "Love, Me" by Collin Raye. As I watched the video play back on national TV, I started crying. I didn't know they were going to add family photos to the performance video. Suddenly everything became so clear to me: we were in the finale *together.*

God had allowed my whole family to be a real part of this journey. My wife and kids were able to experience it all with me. If I hadn't been sent home because of the pandemic, none of that would have happened. The finale wasn't just a *me* thing; it was a *we* thing. Just like it should be.

And then, when the coaches gave their responses to "Love, Me," I couldn't believe Kelly's words. "If I could sound like a man, like singing," she said, "I would want your voice."[1] Could there be a better compliment?

Later, after I sang "I Can Only Imagine" by MercyMe, Kelly told me I inspired her and that she wanted to come to my church. It seemed like the songs touched her at a soul level. That was a winning moment for me.

BROOKE

Recording that video of "Love, Me" with all of our kids was an all-day thing. Our kids were dressed and ready in the morning, and we finally finished late at night. And in the end, it was perfect. It could have never been accomplished if Todd had been in Los Angeles. It was a special moment for Todd to finish this journey with his family. It was a defining moment for us.

"God, you're so good," I whispered with joy. "This would have never happened if Todd had stayed in Los Angeles, and you knew that. You're using it for our good. You've taken this COVID-19 situation—and all the anxiety and the unknowns— and created a special moment for us as a family."

Watching that video back, it was just a pivotal moment. Warmth, joy, and peace filled me, and at that moment, I felt this could be really big for our family. I knew then that Todd's place on *The Voice* wasn't just about him and the show. It was about God's plans for all of us.

Of course, even in that amazing moment, we were still dealing with real-life kids. By the time Todd did a sound check on "Love, Me," little Winnie, age four, was just done. I had promised my kids everything under the sun if they acted right, because it was a long day. Winnie's my youngest, and she's dramatic, but she just fell asleep as he sang. She didn't throw a fit since she was sleeping, and Todd was able to sing for the performance. It was perfect. The song is filled with a lot of emotion; it's a beautiful song.

When it came time to set up for "I Can Only Imagine," we were running out of time. Because we had so little time, production allowed Eagan to have complete freedom over the set, and he was able to show off his skills.

God also brought Todd home, to Cornerstone, where it all began. Todd was able to sing on the very stage where he started his ministry. And for the song "Love, Me," we set the props up in the youth room where he started as youth pastor. We couldn't have designed that if we had tried. I believe God handpicked every song and had a hand in every part of this.

I'm so thankful that Todd didn't limit himself to only singing Christian songs on the show. People got to know Todd and who he was as a person. People who might have been turned off if he'd only sung Christian songs were hooked on his joy. And then, when he sang "I Can Only Imagine" for the finale, viewers got to see where his joy comes from.

God brought everything back full circle. On the final night, our family and closest friends and church members gathered at the church, waiting to find out the results. They held the confetti poppers; their excitement was palpable. But Todd and I knew we were winners either way. I was okay. I knew Todd was okay. In fact, he spent the commercial break telling our kids not to cry when they announced someone else as the winner. And when Carson Daly announced Todd's name, we lost it. Kids were screaming, they were crying with joy, and I was doing some of both myself.

There are very few times in life when you get a perfect moment, but that moment . . . it was just perfect. I know now to save and cherish those moments. They are like memorials—moments I'll tell my kids' kids about.

As our family and friends gathered around us, I realized that the people who'd been with us through the valleys—our parents and siblings, our church, our friends—were now with us for this mountaintop experience. God kept his word that no bad thing would happen. He kept his promise. And he will continue to keep his promises.

That moment, with us all celebrating together, reminded me of a scripture that someone gave me during a really rough season of my life: "Those who sow with tears will reap with songs of joy" (Ps. 126:5).

Brooke, Jesus still whispers to me in quiet moments, *you sowed a lot of tears, a lot of heartache, a lot of pain. And now you're reaping a lot of joy.* It's just so wonderfully overwhelming to me.

Many people say they wish Todd would've done this earlier. I don't think Todd was ready. I wasn't ready either. I think there was a lot that God had to do in our lives before he took us on this venture.

I know this man, but it's cool for the world to get to connect with Todd. Folks like to see that regular people can do extraordinary things, because then they believe that maybe they can do them too. Hope and joy reach further than we ever think—deep into people's hearts.

Now, with the win behind us, God's having to teach me how to be in this new season. I'm not used to this. I'm used to the old. To be honest, he's taking me out of a poverty mentality. For so long I've thought, *It's not going to work out, the bad thing is going to happen*, or, *We better use all this while we can because it'll be gone.* We don't have to walk in fear that this is all going away tomorrow. Instead, we can open our hearts to this new season and whatever God wants to do in it.

There's a new type of transformation that's taking place in me. God is teaching me that even when things were hard, he's been there all along. Our family has always been surrounded by the goodness of God, even when we couldn't see it or feel it. All of this—the valleys and the mountaintops—has been part of his story written for us.

TODD

Through everything God has done in the last year, I feel there's a lot of redemption taking place. A lot of beauty is coming out of the ashes. The scripture I would say is my life scripture is Colossians 3:12: "Therefore, as the elect of God, holy and beloved, put on tender mercies, kindness, humility, meekness, longsuffering" (NKJV). Sometimes our suffering is long, but it's our job to continue to have tender mercy, to be kind, to try to stay humble, to be meek.

Another scripture I've preached often is Psalm 27:13: "I will see the goodness of the LORD in the land of the living." I grew up with everybody just waiting to die, knowing that heaven was the place where there would be no more tears and no more sorrow. It's not that they wanted to die anytime soon. It's just that, as a kid, it seemed to me that everyone was so busy thinking about meeting on the "bountiful shore" in heaven that they didn't pay much attention to the present.

You know, I'll remember the whole goal is to go to heaven and not to hell. But really, the more I live now, I know it's God's will for us to live in his goodness. And I'm experiencing God's goodness in ways I never thought possible.

I still think it's funny when people think I'm somebody special. It's a blast, really, when people stop me and want to meet me or have a picture taken with me. And then there are insane things, like the government of the State of Mississippi making a proclamation about me—about my win. It's framed, and they presented it to me in session. Who would have thought something like that could have happened?

Even in the music industry, I've been able to meet amazing people and make connections. Musicians and producers have gone out of their way to be kind to me. Then there are these people driving hours and hours to come to my shows. The fact that I was doing live music in Pigeon Forge, when no one else was doing live music, was a miracle.

People even brought me cookies to the show. Some ladies from Georgia brought me peaches. There are folks who've made home-made shirts that said "God's Todd" and wore them to the show.

I want to be real honest that I'm certain there are people in the world who will read this and say, "Well, he wasn't that kind to me." Because I know I've messed up—a lot. Still, I've done what I could, and I've always tried to show up. I've tried to be kind to people and just love people and let people know that I love them. And I'm trying to remember that I don't deserve any of this.

Some people have told me that I seemed so professional on the show, but at every moment, I felt like I was treading water. I just did what everyone told me to the best I could.

Remember, this whole thing happened to someone who had not yet released any of his own music. More than that, because of COVID-19, the show drew in different kinds of viewers. Lots of people have told me that they never really watched *The Voice* before, but that I inspired them. They kept watching me, and then they voted. And they came to stand in line at the theater after the show just to talk to me for a few minutes and get a photo. Sometimes I think, *I'm really just a run-of-the-mill guy, and y'all are standing in line to just talk to me?*

People in the parking lot at Sam's Club act like it's bothering me if they say hi. Why would it bother me? I'm just a guy who's blessed to sing songs. I haven't really done any great exploits in the world. In fact, I've considered my life mostly unremarkable—until I pause and consider all the wins I've had.

———•◆•———

I have a super high-maintenance wife (which is what Brooke calls herself) and a whole lot of kids, and I'm singing songs, and that's pretty much the whole deal. On *The Voice*, I put in a lot of effort to sing and do well, but it's really all the people who won. They are the ones who voted. They are the ones in the "TEAM TODD" group on Facebook. And they are the ones who act like, no matter how crappy a sound quality they get on Facebook, they've heard something that's the best thing ever.

Just a year ago, no one really gave me a passing glance. The change overwhelms me, in a good way, and I hope the awe of it never grows old. I hope I'll always have a sense of gratitude for those who enjoy hearing me sing and who say my hope and my joy inspires them.

In this season, God is giving me a chance to be a representative for him. It's not my job to defend the faith. It's my job to just live my life, sing my songs, and let people know that I love them. I'll take that win.

WINS FOR TODAY

✓ We win when we discover good comes out of hard seasons.

✓ We win when we choose to be grateful.

✓ We win when we understand that sometimes God chooses us to bring hope to others.

✓ We win when we can be trusted with the small things.

✓ We win when we realize God's plan is always a *we* thing, not a *me* thing.

✓ We win when we trust that, after sowing tears, we will reap joy.

✓ We win when we understand that both the valleys and the mountains are part of God's story for us.

✓ We win when we discover the goodness of God where we least expect it.

CHAPTER 13

Next Chapters . . . and Your Story

TODD

The final minutes of season 18 of *The Voice* came down to Carson Daly announcing the winner. The tension for us, the three finalists, and our families—who were all simultaneously on camera and being broadcast to the millions of viewers—was palpable. Then Carson announced . . . a commercial break.

I used the break to take a big breath, but also to remind my kids about how to respond when the winner was announced. "Remember, we're all going to smile and be excited for the winner," I told them. "No crying or looking sad. We're going to clap and celebrate for whoever it is."

But the winner was me.

That moment seemed like the perfect moment, an "I love you" from God. Brooke felt from the very beginning that God promised her that this experience with *The Voice* would be good. And he was true to his promise.

Like when we were married and when our children were born, this win was a moment of pure joy. It was also just the first step. This win has expanded our congregation. Many people are reaching out, wanting the hope and joy that Brooke and I have.

"Why do you do what you do?" people ask. "Why do you have so many kids? How do you make it work in your home? How does your marriage operate? Where does all that joy come from? Why do you love Jesus?"

Brooke and I love sharing our stories because we know how the stories of others have helped us. Stories are powerful in doing that.

One of my most favorite quotes of all time is by Norman Maclean from the book *A River Runs Through It*: "Eventually, all things merge into one, and a river runs through it. The river was cut by the world's great flood and runs over rocks from the basement of time. On some of the rocks are timeless raindrops. Under the rocks are the words, and some of the words are theirs."[1]

The river is time. It just keeps moving. It considers nothing and no one. It just marches on. None of our stories can last forever, but our stories can make an indelible mark. Our stories can remain on the rocks forever, even though the river never stops. Time will go on, but we are the ones who get to decide if we're willing to let God write his stories with our lives.

For a while, I allowed other people to write my story. I spent a lot of years just feeling like everybody expected me to do certain things. I tried to live as people thought I should. Sometimes I still feel an innate need to explain myself so people won't be upset with me. And let me say this: I believe that God is sovereign. I feel like one way or the other, I was where I was supposed to be. But a lot of my decisions came from worry and feelings of personal responsibility. That was wrong of me. It was pride, really. I believed that people relied on me to do the right thing. I also believed that they would struggle or suffer if I wasn't there.

What I realize even more now is that no matter how hard I work, I can't be everything to everybody. They need Jesus for that. My job is to simply live my story. To seek God. To follow him. To take steps of faith. And to trust.

Right now, you might not like your story very much. I understand. The chapter you're in the middle of might be the worst one ever. But believe that if you turn to God, he can do something with it. A beautiful story can emerge, even when there are struggles and conflicts along the way. In fact, the overcoming of those things is what makes stories beautiful.

When you think about it, it's hard to believe that good stories have come from all that's been hard or has gone wrong in our lives. It's a miracle that Brooke and I are okay. That we're not divorced. That we have all these kids. And that we've survived and sometimes thrived. It's a miracle because of all the things we've been through—all the things every family goes through.

It's really important to me that if I am going to be a voice in anybody's life, it would be a calming, reassuring, and encouraging one. A voice that says, "It's going to be all right. God cares. God is there." Personally, I feel like I'm able to minister to more people now than I ever have, and that's part of this new chapter that God is writing.

Over the years, God has brought redemption through healing some of our relationships, as we've learned to forgive and are forgiven. Because of my participation in *The Voice*, Brooke and I have even been able to reconnect with some of the relationships that were broken. Only God can do that.

As I stood before Cornerstone Church not too long ago, preaching for the last time, I told them I was thankful that God chose me to do this—to be their pastor. God could have done anything with anybody. He probably could have done more with other people, and it's remarkable he chose me. And I love that he's now allowing me to take Cornerstone into the world. As I told my church, "You might be able to take the boy out of Cornerstone, but no one's going to be able to take Cornerstone out of the boy."

Between my daddy and me, that's twenty-eight years of leading that church. But in truth, we were the ones changed. I have seen God move in my life in a million different ways, and I've read in Scripture another million ways he has moved and worked, and not one time have I ever seen him change anything for the worse. Never. He always changes things for the better. Always.

Just as a confirmation that I am following God with the right steps, the day after our going-away service at Cornerstone, a box showed up in the mail. It was my trophy—my award—for winning *The Voice*. And it showed up six months after my win. It was a reminder from God that he's giving me this platform, and that I need to continue to follow him.

With this new platform of music, God has given me another way to share his love. Yes, people may enjoy my voice, but they also are drawn to the joy and hope I share. Both of which come from God alone.

As I'm leaving full-time church ministry, some people have said, "I thought God called you to pastor." And I answer, "He did. And I did."

Through my role as a pastor, my goal has always been summed up as this: to free people from the prison of perfection and also to challenge them to love like Jesus. This isn't done by pounding the pulpit, spitting, and shouting—although I have been known to get loud and excited when I preach. But instead, I've always tried to make the God of the Bible relatable to ordinary people and our everyday circumstances. I want them to know that to choose him is to win.

People need to know that no matter where they are in life, God is right there with them, and he cares. And this will be my goal with my music too. To help people know that Jesus accepts us just as we are. We don't have to clean ourselves up to come to him. And when we do come to him, he has a story written for our lives. A story he wants us to live and share with others. We can depend on his love, live in his love, and then share his love. Our job is as simple as that, and to just take the next step.

Brooke did have to push me to be on *The Voice*, like she did with so many other things. But with the next steps in my life, I'm stepping out in confidence. As hard as it was, the time of my full-time pastoring had to end. God has done so much, and I'm following him in faith and giving music a shot. He's opening doors that I never thought would open, and he's giving me favor within the music industry, which is simply amazing.

My faith has grown. How could it not after this experience? Currently, we've moved to Tennessee, closer to Nashville, and in this decision, Brooke didn't have to push. I believe that God is good. I believe that this music thing can go somewhere. I'm finally making up my own mind to take a leap of faith as the leader of our family. And that is a win.

———◆———

Going back to the song that I sang for my open-call audition, these words speak to my heart: "Seen my share of broken halos. Folded wings that used to fly." The good news is that when it comes to the Lord, he can use broken halos and folded wings. Things don't have to end there.

No one can go through life without messing up. Each of us will have broken halos. Each of us will fold our wings, afraid to open them. Afraid to soar. Yet the real victory isn't when we achieve great things. Instead, it's the little wins in everyday life that lead to victory. It's being willing to forgive and to seek forgiveness. It's deciding to open your home and heart to more kids, even though you already feel stretched to the limit. It's trusting in the gifts God has given you and daring to believe in his good plans for your life. It's refusing to allow the darkness to overwhelm you, and instead looking to the light of God again and again.

When I started this journey, I had no idea what the end result would be, but that result is truly this: God took my voice to the sick and the lonely. He's allowing me to still do that now.

When pastors say it's important to live by faith, mostly we're preaching to ourselves. Sometimes that includes getting back up when we fall down; that's part of our faith, you know? Nowhere in the Bible does it say that a righteous man doesn't fall. Instead, Proverbs says: "For though the righteous fall seven times, they rise again" (24:16).

To me, that is the demonstration of our faith. That when we fall, we can rise again. *When* we fall, because we will. The point isn't being worried about falling again; it's getting up.

I've spent way too much of my life worrying about falling. Now I'm doing the next step of my life unafraid. That's what faith is. I have always been the one to preach to the congregation that God takes you to those places that are uncomfortable, and you have to do the uncomfortable things sometimes. Now I'm preaching to myself—and to you. I wasn't too old. It wasn't too late. You're not too old. It's not too late.

What are your dreams? Do they seem out of reach? Good. That is exactly where God wants you to be. Have faith and say *yes* to God. He will open the right doors at the right time for the right things. He will propel you into your purpose. If you truly have a heart for God, and a heart for his people, God will use that for good.

Don't be afraid to share your story—all of it—the fears and the joy. There is someone out there who needs to hear your words today, or maybe hear your song. The world needs your voice. Remember that.

And then there's one final thing: man, I love y'all. Remember that too.

WINS FOR TODAY

- ✓ We win when we discover that in God's economy, brokenness leads to beauty, and scarcity to abundance.
- ✓ We win when we don't try to hide from what God wants to do in our lives.
- ✓ We win when we discover that on the other side of fear is freedom, and with freedom comes joy.
- ✓ We win when we discover that God desires to use all our stories and all our voices.

"Still to Come"
by Todd Tilghman

I've been told it's temporary
And I'm trying to hang on
And they tell me don't get weary
And they say don't lose your song
It's not that I'm afraid the storm will last
It's the things that might get lost along its path
And I wish that I could tell you
What's on the other side of the mountain
Without the climb

[Chorus]
But the glory's still to come
Despite what I see now
The clouds are sure to break
Even if I don't know how
And I know I'm not alone fighting the fear, fighting the doubt
And I know the end is not what I see now
'Cause the glory's still to come

One foot in front of the other
Even crawling if I must
Every moment I surrender
There's more beauty from the dust
So I'm giving all I have and all I am
And when I've done all I can do, that's when I'll stand
And I wish that I could tell you
What's on the other side of the mountain
Without the climb

[Chorus]

And this suffering's not forever
And this pain is not for nothing
Every moment of my breaking
Has its purpose; it has meaning
And I wish that I could tell you
What's on the other side of the mountain
Without the climb

[Chorus]

Acknowledgments

Thank you, Janet Grant, for being a wonderful agent, holding our hands along the way. Our publisher, Nelson Books, has been amazing to work with. We are deeply indebted to Jenny Baumgartner and Sujin Hong on the editorial team. We would also like to thank Karen Jackson, Sara Broun, Shea Nolen, and Claire Drake on the marketing and publicity team.

We are ever thankful for our kids. We also want to show appreciation to our families:

My mom and dad, Clarence and Teresa
My brother, Chad, and his family
My sister, Holly, and her family
Brooke's mom and dad, Doug and Jan
Brooke's brother, Shaun, and his wife
Brooke's sister, Melanie, and her family

ACKNOWLEDGMENTS

Thank you to the wonderful people of Cornerstone Church, past and present, who shaped us into the people we are.

Finally, I truly appreciate NBC, *The Voice*, and Blake Shelton for taking a chance.

Notes

CHAPTER 3: MINISTRY MINDED

1. Rebecca Turner, "Brooke Tilghman, Wife of 'The Voice' Winner, Joins Good Things," October 21, 2020, in *Good Things*, SuperTalk Mississippi, video, 13:03, https://www.supertalk.fm/brooke -tilghman-wife-of-the-voice-winner-joins-good-things/.

CHAPTER 6: THE VALLEY OF THE SHADOW OF DEATH

1. Romans 12:2: "Do not conform to the pattern of this world, but be transformed by the renewing of your mind."

CHAPTER 9: GOING VIRAL

1. Brooke Tilghman (@brooke.tilghman), Facebook, August 25, 2017, https://www.facebook.com/brooke.tilghman/posts /10154871182028027.
2. *Making It*, season 2, episode 2, "Ordinary Home to Extraordinary Home," hosted by Amy Poehler and Nick Offerman, aired December 3, 2019, NBC, video, 29:25, https://www.nbc.com /making-it/video/ordinary-home-to-extraordinary-home/4075920.

3. Eagan talked about his parents supporting his dreams on the show *Making It*. However, this quote is from Blake McMillan, "The Tilghman NBC Thing: Father and Son Both on Television," *The Tack*, May 11, 2020, bvtack.com/33120/arts-life/the-tilghman -nbc-thing-father-and-son-both-on-television/.

4. *Making It*, season 2, episode 5, "Work and Play," aired December 9, 2019, NBC, video, 41:55, https://www.nbc.com/making-it /video/work-and-play/4079256.

CHAPTER 11: ROAD TO *THE VOICE*

1. *The Voice* Casting (@thevoicecasting), Instagram video, May 20, 2020, https://www.instagram.com/p/CAbZXoVl2oU/ ("WINNER, WINNER! CONGRATULATIONS @todd_tilghman!! We knew you were a STAR since the moment we saw you in Atlanta! #TheVoice #TheVoiceCasting").

2. *The Voice* Casting (@thevoicecasting), Instagram video.

3. "Todd Tilghman—Bob Seger & The Silver Bullet Band's 'We've Got Tonight'—Voice Blind Auditions" (Los Angeles), featuring Kelly Clarkson, John Legend, Nick Jonas, and Blake Shelton, aired February 24, 2020, NBC, video shared by *The Voice*, YouTube, https://www.youtube.com/watch?v=0hDuvlrJ2I8&list =PLlYqpJ9JE-J-LeqAYInEgJ2sV5eO5x3zf&ab_channel=TheVoice.

4. *The Voice*, season 18, episode 8, "The Battles, Part 3," featuring Kelly Clarkson, John Legend, Nick Jonas, and Blake Shelton, aired April 6, 2020, NBC.

5. "Jon Mullins vs. Todd Tilghman—Shenandoah's 'Ghost in This House'—The Voice Battles 2020" (Los Angeles), featuring Kelly Clarkson, John Legend, Nick Jonas, and Blake Shelton, aired April 6, 2020, NBC, video shared by *The Voice*, YouTube, 4:02, https://www.youtube.com/watch?v=CV6pi1FDUAE &ab_channel=TheVoice.

6. "James Taylor as the Mega Mentor on NBC's The Voice" (Los Angeles), featuring Kelly Clarkson, John Legend, Nick Jonas, and Blake Shelton, aired April 13, 2020, NBC, video shared by *The Voice*, YouTube, 3:02, https://www.youtube.com /watch?v=80KlHLvkaMY.

CHAPTER 12: MINOR DISAPPOINTMENTS, MAJOR VICTORIES

1. "Todd Tilghman Performs the Collin Raye Song 'Love, Me'—The Voice Top 9 Performances 2020" (Meridian, MS), featuring Kelly Clarkson, John Legend, Nick Jonas, and Blake Shelton, aired May 11, 2020, NBC, video shared by *The Voice*, YouTube, 3:05, https://www.youtube.com/watch?v=nrBKpyllv3k&ab_channel=TheVoice.

CHAPTER 13: NEXT CHAPTERS . . . AND YOUR STORY

1. Norman Maclean, *A River Runs Through It* (Chicago: University of Chicago Press, 1976), 161.

About the Authors

Parents of eight, Todd and Brooke Tilghman currently live in Tennessee, moving closer to Nashville for Todd's leap of faith to pursue music full time. From 2011 to 2020, Todd was the pastor of Cornerstone Church in Meridian, Mississippi. He has the distinction of being the oldest winner, at age forty-two, in *The Voice*'s history. Todd has been singing in church since he was eight years old, and he is currently writing and recording songs for his first album, to be released in 2021. Brooke continues to cheer him on.

USA Today bestselling author Tricia Goyer has published eighty books, has written more than five hundred articles for national publications, and is on the blogging team at TheBetterMom.com and other homeschooling and Christian websites. She is a two-time Carol Award winner, a Christy and ECPA Award finalist, and regularly receives starred reviews in *Romantic Times* and *Publishers Weekly*. Tricia is a wife to John, a mom to ten kids, and a Nana to a growing number of grandkids. Connect with her at TriciaGoyer.com.